troduction

o

HONOLOGICAL

HEORY

BERT T. HARMS

Introduction to
PHONOLOGICAL THEORY

Prentice-Hall International, Inc., *London*
Prentice-Hall of Australia, Pty. Ltd., *Sydney*
Prentice-Hall of Canada, Ltd., *Toronto*
Prentice-Hall of India Private Ltd., *New Delhi*
Prentice-Hall of Japan, Inc., *Tokyo*

Introduction to
PHONOLOGICAL THEORY))

ROBERT T. HARMS

Department of Linguistics
The University of Texas at Austin

PRENTICE-HALL, INC.

Englewood Cliffs, New Jersey

Library of Congress Catalog Card Number 68–25909
Printed in the United States of America

Current Printing (last digit):

10 9 8 7 6 5 4 3 2 1

SIRPALLE

Preface

Generative phonology is currently in a state of rapid development. New proposals affecting nearly every aspect of this approach are found in increasing frequency. The linguistic community as a whole, however, has not had ready access to the basic discussions concerning the assumptions and conventions of this important area of linguistic study. What should have been a vital part of any linguistic program has often been neglected for the lack of suitable introductory materials. This manual, developed in conjunction with phonology courses at The University of Texas at Austin, does not pretend to give final answers to the many problems of generative phonology; its goal is to provide a basis for understanding many of the fundamental issues now being discussed. It is presented in the hope that the reader will himself become an active participant.

The reader is assumed to have a certain familiarity with articulatory phonetics, some notion of the phonemic principle (see, for example, Sapir, 1925, 1951; Jakobson and Halle, 1956; Jakobson, Fant, and Halle, 1951), and a limited acquaintance with the workings of transformational grammar (see Bach, 1964, Chomsky, 1965). The Jakobsonian distinctive features have been presented solely from an articulatory point of view, and no attempt is made to explain the acoustic basis of the features (for this the reader is referred to Jakobson, Fant, and Halle, 1951, Halle, 1959).

A preliminary version of this book has been used in an undergraduate first course in phonology, following phonetics and a general introduction to linguistics. The exercises are designed to force the reader to come to grips with the relevant chapters of the text and in places even to suggest revisions of the basic theory. One should not seek the strictly correct solution, but rather the answer that offers the most reasonable explanation of the data. The data for the exercises have been taken from numerous sources, relatively few of them generative, and although the term 'phoneme' is used, one should question whether the same relationships will obtain at the systematic phonemic level. Numerous qualifications on the data in the source materials have been omitted in preparing the exercises (such as exceptions to general rules), but it is my opinion that the phenomena thus simplified still reflect valid processes in the given languages. Used as a textbook the exercises provide ample assignment materials for a full semester of work.

I wish to express my gratitude to numerous colleagues and students for their encouragment and suggestions. I am specially indebted to James D. McCawley, whose influence is reflected throughout this work, for introducing me to the procedures of generative phonology through personal correspondence and his numerous unpublished papers; to Emmon Bach, whose stimulation lead to the preparation of this text; and to Donald A. Becker and Eugene E. Loos, who tested many of the ideas presented here in their dissertations, for many valuable insights.

ROBERT T. HARMS

Contents

ix

Introduction to
PHONOLOGICAL THEORY

CHAPTER 1

Introduction

The domain of generative phonology may be defined very broadly as those components of generative grammar which serve to provide the phonetic representations of utterances in any given language. Thus it includes the phonological form of morphemes and morphs listed in the lexicon—also those inserted via certain rules, the morpheme-structure rule component (Chapter 8), and the phonological rule component (Chapter 9). Ultimately, however, generative phonology seeks to provide a general theory explaining the competence of the native speaker in the sounds of his language. The purpose of this book is to shed light on the workings of generative phonology as currently practised, and also to give some insight into the problem of how the explanatory aspects of phonology are related to its formal devices.

The fundamental unit of generative phonology is the distinctive feature, although various nonphonological features, boundary symbols, and syntactic bracketing also play an important role. The phoneme—specifically, the systematic phoneme—has a clearly secondary status, but, for matters of presentation, it is frequently convenient to refer to phonemes as the underlying segments used to designate or 'spell' morphemes—i.e., segments containing the minimum number of distinctive feature-specifications required to account for the phonetic realization of the morphemes. However, owing to the fact that certain phonological features are seen to be redundant when we consider their position of occurrence, the number of features in various lexical instances of the 'same' phoneme may be different in relation to its environment; for example, the /s/ in /sin/ contains approximately five more feature-specifications than the /s/ in /spin/ since initially before an obstruent, the only possible consonant in native English words is /s/, and most of the distinctive features of this latter /s/ can thus be supplied by a rule (a 'sequential-constraint' rule, cf. Chapter 8) and need not be specified in the lexical listing of such morphemes. A somewhat more precise definition of the systematic phoneme may be given as:

> One of the set of segments that contain only distinctively specified features —and from which no distinctive feature-specifications have been deleted by virtue of environmental (sequential-constraint) redundancies—and that underlie the segments actually used to designate morphemes.

Thus, although the /s/'s in /sin/, /spin/, and /pæst/ contain different feature-specifications in their lexical listings, they may all be said to represent the single phoneme /s/.

The phonemes of a language are generally listed as a matrix of classificatory features, showing which features must be distinctively specified for each phoneme. For example,

	i	e	a	o	u
flat	−	−	−	+	+
low	−	−	+		
high	+	−		−	+

But it must be kept in mind that such charts are merely devices for presenting the underlying distinctive phonological relationships of the language, and do not form a part of the phonological theory of any language. The classificatory matrix thus indicates the optimal feature specification of each phoneme segment, apart from considerations of sequential-constraint redundancy.

Instead of 'phonemic', the term 'underlying' is frequently used. In citing forms, the use of slashes /   / is generally reserved for underlying representations; brackets [   ]—for any lower-level representation (i.e., one to which one or more rules have applied), although upon occasion the slashes are used merely to set off a form that is relatively close to the underlying shape of the morpheme string. Where a form in brackets does not approximate its phonetic output (pronunciation), it is desirable that this fact should be clear from context (generally by indicating the eventual pronunciation as '> [   ]').

Since phonological rules can refer to morpheme features, morphological boundaries, and syntactic bracketing, it is readily apparent that generative phonology cannot be properly understood without some knowledge of the other components of the grammar.

The system of generative grammar assumed in this presentation is essentially that of Noam Chomsky's *Aspects of the Theory of Syntax* (1965). The following components are relevant:

1. the base, consisting of
   (a) the base rules,
   (b) the lexicon,
2. the semantic component,
3. the transformational component.

The base rules assign each sentence ('S') an underlying ('deep') structure. In part, this is in the form of a constituent-structure tree diagram; for example, the following tree may be said to underly the sentence 'the old man lifted the fish':

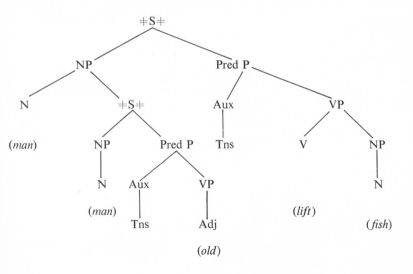

The terminal nodes of the tree are subsequently developed through the use of features; e.g., the leftmost N node will be assigned the features '+ Noun, + Definite, + Count, − Plural, + Animate, + Human'; the Tns node of the sentence, which is dominated by (which hangs from) the first NP, will be '+ Present'; the V node will be specified as having a subject which contains the features listed above for the leftmost N node, etc.

The lexicon attaches given morphemes to the terminal nodes of the structure provided by the base rules. These morphemes must be in harmony with the features present at each node. Thus 'fish' could not be attached to the leftmost N node because it is not '+ Human'. Each morpheme will be in the form of a distinctive feature matrix, indicating its underlying representation. It will also contain information required for the semantic component (e.g., its 'meaning'), the transformational component (e.g., features which call for or block the application of given rules—'+ T10, − T13'), and the phonological components (e.g., the information that it is a recent loanword—a feature such as '+ Foreign'). In the case of 'fish' in the example sentence, if it is marked as '+ plural' by the base rules, the lexicon will need a rule feature to prevent it from inserting an '− s' plural morph (via a later transformational rule), but the fact of its being plural would be passed along to the semantic component.

The output of the base is subsequently processed in two essentially independent components. On the one hand, the semantic component provides it with a semantic interpretation ('reading'); any information relevant to this semantic reading must, then, stem from the base. On the other hand, the deep-structure string must undergo certain transformational changes and receive a pronounceable form before it can be recognized as a sentence of English. The Adj 'old' must be shifted to a position before the leftmost N, and all other elements of the sentence dominated by the NP must be deleted. The definite nouns 'man' and 'fish' require the insertion of the definite article 'the'. Note, however, that no information relevant to the semantic interpretation of the sentence may be added or deleted. The sentence could not be made passive unless the base rules had added the element 'Passive' to its deep structure. The remaining Tns node, which is '+ Past', is realized as '-ed' and shifted to the right side of the verb as a suffix. The result of these transformational changes, in addition to subsequent restructuring, provides a tree such as the following, where conventional orthography is used for purposes of illustration:

‡ S ‡

NP — PredP

(the) Adj N — VP

(old) (man)

V — NP

(lift) (ed) (the) N

(fish)

In the syntactic components, the basic unit is the entire morpheme, not individual phoneme segments; thus,

‡⁀the⁀old⁀man⁀lift⁀ed⁀the⁀fish⁀‡

where each item of the string is separated by the concatenation symbol '⁀', although the concatenation sign is normally not indicated before or after boundary symbols. Once the phrase (|), word, (‡), and morpheme (+) boundaries are inserted by late transformational rules, the string becomes

|the‡old‡man‡lift+ed‡the‡fish|

Finally, as the string enters the domain of the phonological component, the concatenated elements of the string become, by general convention, the individual segments of the morphemes; thus, using unit phoneme symbols for simplicity of illustration,

|ð⁀i‡o⁀l⁀d‡m⁀æ⁀n‡l⁀i⁀f⁀t+d‡ð⁀i‡f⁀i⁀š|

The syntactic bracketing and nonphonological features of given morphemes are also retained, so that the sentence illustrated above contains substantially more information than is indicated by the phonemic transcription.

Thus all phonological rules operate on segments of given morphemes—either individual morphemes (from the lexicon, or inserted transformationally) or strings of morphemes in utterances.

CHAPTER 2

The Choice of a Universal Phonetic System

Nearly all approaches to phonemics assume the existence of some kind of universal phonetic 'alphabet', generally consisting of a set of alphabetic symbols together with various diacritical markings—such as the I.P.A. system, the transcription system of the Finno-Ugric Society, or the one presented by Bloch and Trager in their *Outline of Linguistic Analysis*—or phonetic feature notations, such as those developed by Roman Jakobson, or by Kenneth Pike in his *Phonetics*.

Beyond the obvious goal of describing the phonetic data of natural languages, a universal phonetic theory must also seek to formulate universal constraints on feature co-occurrence and feature contrasts. Of the more recent phonetic systems, that of Jakobson and those developed from it have been explicitly concerned with the discovery of such general laws. One way of stating these constraints is to formulate hypotheses about possible combinations of features; for example, that vowel phonemes will not contrast in voicing, or that if a language has only two high vowel phonemes, one will be a front unrounded vowel and the other a back rounded vowel.

A second way involves the complementary distribution of various related gross phonetic features that may be considered realizations of a single feature in the universal set; for example, rounding, pharyngealization, and retroflexion are represented by the single feature 'flat'. This grouping is the equivalent of a hypothesis to the effect that no language will have two phonemes that contrast solely in terms of these gross phonetic features (e.g., a contrast of retroflex and labialized *t*, or a contrast of labiovelar and pharyngealized *k*).

Sometimes these universal constraints can be inferred more indirectly. A contrast of the labiodental [v] and the bilabial [β] can be handled by the feature of stridence (relative degree of friction), but not by articulatory position, since the features grave, compact, etc., serve only to distinguish labials in general, without further specification, such as labiodental or bilabial articulation. Thus no feature is available to describe the difference between a bilabial [m] or [b] and a labiodental [ɱ] or [ḇ]. This amounts to a prediction that no phonemic bilabial : labiodental contrast will be found among the labial nasals or stops, but that it may occur among the fricatives, as for Ewe /β/ : /v/.

Other phonetic systems, with and without features, could also serve as a basis for such general laws, but at the moment no other phonetic system has been sufficiently well developed to compete seriously with those based upon the distinctive-feature approach of Jakobson. Jakobsonian phonology, however, is essentially a taxonomic approach, and the use of Jakobsonian features should not be equated with generative phonology. Further, it is not only the concern of the Jakobsonian phonetic system with universal constraints that has led to its adoption within generative phonology.

First of all, one might ask whether the fundamental units of phonology are indivisible segments like /p/, /o/, etc., or phonetic features like 'voiced', 'nasal', etc. The most compelling argument for the use of features has been given by Morris Halle (1962b). If, for example, we compare the three rules:

(1) a $\longrightarrow$ æ in the environment __i

(2) a $\longrightarrow$ æ in the environment __$\begin{Bmatrix} i \\ e \\ æ \end{Bmatrix}$

(3) a $\longrightarrow$ æ in the environment __$\begin{Bmatrix} i \\ k \\ z \end{Bmatrix}$

it should be apparent that the three rules differ in generality. (2) is more general than (1), since 'before any front vowel' is a more general statement than 'before /i/'. (2) is also more general than (3), since there is a common feature which all the members of (2)'s environment share, but no such feature can be found for the members of the environment of (3), which is only a list of unrelated phonemes. (1) is a more general rule than (3), for essentially the same reason.

If simplicity is measured by counting alphabetic segments, rule (1) would be simpler than rule (2), and rules (2) and (3) would be equally simple. With a feature approach, however, (2) will require fewer features than (1); and (1), fewer features than (3). (A third possibility which might produce the desired result within a segmental approach involves the establishment of general classes, such as front vowels, on an ad hoc basis for each language. But without appeal to some kind of underlying phonetic feature system, the motivation for the choice of the class /i e æ/ as more general than /i k z/ is unclear.)

Ideally, the notion of 'simplicity' in a phonological description will directly reflect the generality of the rules in such a way that the most general rules are those which can ultimately be shown to consist of actual units in the language. Thus, a description with the greatest generality should also be the most economical one; one with the least generality, the least economical. The way in which we count symbols in the phonology (or grammar) should reward those descriptions which are more reasonable hypotheses about the phonological (or grammatical) processes of the languages, and penalize those descriptions which are less reasonable. This approach to relating simplicity to generality so defined is known as the 'simplicity metric'.

The simplicity metric itself is, then, a hypothesis about the nature of language, and must be subject to empirical validation. Proposals for testing various aspects of the simplicity metric in phonology through the phenomena of historical change have been made by Emmon Bach (1966) and Paul Kiparsky (1967b).

The next question that must be answered concerns the preference for binary plus/minus features over other feature approaches (such as that proposed by Hockett, 1955). Consider the two sets of rules:

(4)   nasal ⟶
$\begin{cases} \text{labial in the environment} & \underline{\hspace{1cm}}\text{labial} \\ \text{apical in the environment} & \underline{\hspace{1cm}}\text{apical} \\ \text{dorsal in the environment} & \underline{\hspace{1cm}}\text{dorsal} \end{cases}$

(5)   nasal ⟶
$\begin{cases} \text{labial in the environment} & \underline{\hspace{1cm}}\text{labial} \\ \text{voiceless in the environment} & \underline{\hspace{1cm}}\text{spirant} \end{cases}$

Again the problem of the simplicity metric arises. Clearly, set (4) is a statement of a single general homorganic assimilation of nasals to following consonants. But (5), which covers two unrelated phenomena, would nonetheless be the simpler of the two sets. By using the Jakobsonian features with plus/minus values (together with alpha-type variables; see Rule (viii), Chapter 7, below), Set (4) will require fewer features than (5).

EXERCISES

1. A taxonomic description of Assiniboine presents the following stop-allophone distributions (Levin 1964: 3–9):

phoneme	allophone		in the environment
/p/	[pʰ]	(1)	＿＿á, é (stressed /a e/)
	[b]	(2)	＿＿ă, ĕ, ĭ (unstressed /a e i/)
		(3)	in certain short words before a final ă which is lost
	[p]	(4)	elsewhere
/t/	[d]	(5)	‡＿＿ú, ó, á (‡ is word boundary)
	[tʰ]	(6)	＿＿á, é, í
	[t]	(7)	elsewhere
/k/	[g]	(8)	＿＿ă, ĭ, ŭ
	[kʰ]	(9)	＿＿a, ắ, u, ṹ, o
	[k]	(10)	elsewhere
/c/	[ž]	(11)	＿＿ă, ĕ, ŭ
	[č]	(12)	elsewhere

Assiniboine is said to have the oral vowels /i u e o a/ and nasal vowels /ĩ ũ ã/. Although the 'elsewhere' environments for /p t k/ provide examples only of preconsonantal occurrences of the stops, other forms, such as [ĩkmṹtãga] *lion* and [haiákɛna] *clothes*, can be found under the discussion of other phonemes. The phone [č] does not occur before consonants (except for a glottalized [čʔ]), and is exemplified only before stressed vowels.

(a) In what ways might concern with generality of description lead us to rearrange the above allophone statements?

(b) Considering the fact that the description is based upon limited acquaintance with the language, does the presentation seem suspicious (i.e., make claims contrary to reasonable expectations of phonological behavior)?

(c) Why are such suspicions not likely to be pointed up by the type of approach illustrated by the above presentation?

2. Atsugewi short vowel allophones are described as follows (Olmsted 1958
   215–16):

> '/i/ allophones: [ɪ] before any consonant cluster of which the first
> member is not [ʔ], [i] elsewhere . . . .
> /e/ allophones: [ɛ] before any consonant cluster whose first member is
> not [ʔ], [e] elsewhere . . . .
> /a/ allophones: [a] and [ɐ], in free variation in all positions . . . .
> /o/ allophones: [ɔ] before any consonant cluster whose first member is
> not [ʔ], [o] elsewhere . . . .
> /u/ allophones: [U] before any consonant cluster whose first member
> is not [ʔ], [u] elsewhere . . . .
> /ə/ phone [ə].'

   (a) What significant, but unstated (i.e. left for the reader to discover for
       himself) generalizations are contained in the above passage? Is the
       organization and style of the passage one that compels the reader to see
       all generalizations?
   (b) Given the framework of the above analysis; apart from the facts of
       Atsugewi, would it make any difference if the environment of [U ɛ
       were 'before any consonant cluster whose first member is not [p]'?

3. In his analysis of the Atsugewi long vowels, Olmsted concludes (1958
   216):

> 'Hence, though for reasons of "economy" (reducing the sheer number of
> items in the phonemic inventory) they are here regarded as composed
> of the short vowel plus /·/, a phoneme of length, it turns out that they
> are best regarded for other purposes (e.g., calculating phonemic distri-
> butions) as six entirely different "phonemic bundles".'

   (a) Compare the notion of 'economy' suggested here and the economy of
       the simplicity metric. What is the explanatory value of 'economy' in the
       above passage? Is it a hypothesis about the phonological structure of
       language?
   (b) How does 'calculating phonemic distributions' weigh as a factor here?
   (c) What are the implications of adding devices such as / · / to the
       inventory of phonemes? How might this device be expressed within
       a distinctive-feature approach?

4. A consideration of the phonemic status of Toba-Batak [o] and and [ɔ],
   which do not contrast in any given utterance frame, but which require
   complicated rules to account for their respective occurrences, leads
   Percival (1960: 385–86) to conclude:

> 'In our Toba-Batak example the two solutions admitted by the defini-
> tion of the phoneme differ in one important respect: one requires a

complete listing of the environments of the allophones, the other does not. The former solution is therefore more complicated than the latter. ... Economy is not a matter of the number of phonemes set up, but a function of the number of rules required to state the relations between the phonemic and allophonic levels.'

(a) Compare this notion of economy with that expressed above by Olmsted, and with the economy of the simplicity metric.

(b) In Southern Paiute, [č] and [c] do not contrast, and a general rule can be provided to account for their occurrence. To consider them as separate phonemes does not require additional rules in the phonology. Would Percival's economy lead to the desired analysis in this instance?

CHAPTER 3

Systematic Phonemics
and Systematic Phonetics

All recent phonological systems that use alphabetical segments employ the same symbols for phonemes as for phones; e.g., /m/ and [m]. The same is true of the use of the features in generative phonology. Both approaches also emphasize the necessity for distinguishing the role of the phonemic-level symbols from that of the phonetic-level symbols.

In generative phonology, as well as in certain taxonomic systems, the features that define phonemes are not considered different in nature from the features which occur in phonetic segments; e.g., for a vowel phoneme that is distinctively compact and realized by compact phones, the feature of compactness is not regarded as a different entity on the two levels. In a sense, this is the basis for the taxonomic-phonemic criterion of phonetic similarity in the grouping of allophones; (those taxonomic systems which lack this criterion would not be similar to generative phonology here; e.g., Harris, 1951, cf. Chapter 7.) In neither approach is there an effective discovery procedure that leads from the phonetic corpus to the best phonemic system. Least of all can an appeal to acoustic measurements of the data be decisive in determining the number or nature of phonemic oppositions in the language.

The primary aims of generative phonology are to provide a phonemic representation of morphemes and a series of ordered rules that, together with information about boundary phenomena (junctures), (1) adequately express the phonological generalizations of the language and (2) at the same time determine the phonetic form of all utterances in the language.

Note that nothing has been said about the simplicity (or economy) of the resultant system. Simplicity, as noted above, can not be considered apart from the notion of generality, which is basic here. The role of the simplicity metric is to devise a method of counting the elements present in the morphemes and rules in such a way that the more highly valued phonological system for a given language (in terms of its generality) will always be the more economical one. Thus the simplicity metric forces the analysis in the direction of greater generality, and, given two or more alternative solutions, will lead to the choice of the most desirable one. Discovering the best approach in the first place, however, is left to the insight and ingenuity of the analyst, aided, perhaps, by the intuition of the native speaker. The underlying representations of morphemes as well as the phonological rules necessarily require information of a nonphonetic nature, information to which native speakers have access, i.e., the meanings of morphemes, syntactic structure, and whether given morphemes are regular or irregular, normal native forms or special in some sense.

In the use of the features, however, a sharp distinction remains between the phonological processes of the language and those which require nonphonological information. Neither phonetic contrasts nor phonetic features should be employed to cover up such information. For example, in Finnish, /v/ and /p/ are separate phonemes (cf. /vala/ *oath*, /pala/ *piece*). In closed syllables, /p/ is realized as [v] via a general rule which 'weakens' intervocalic stops; e.g., /kalvo/ *membrane*, with /v/, has the genitive /kalvon/ = [kalvon], and /halpa/ *cheap* has the genitive /halpan/ = [halvan]. Although the phonemic representations require the knowledge that the one morpheme has a nominative with a /p/ and the other with a /v/, the [v] of [halvan] is nonetheless the result of a general phonological process. To list two phonemic allomorphs /halpa/ ∼ /halva/ would amount to treating them as some kind of suppletion, and would obscure the generalization involved here. Yet certain classes of morphemes, such as recent loans and proper nouns, do not undergo the general rule; e.g., /valpo/ *State Police* has the genitive [valpon]. To describe this [p], which does not undergo the above rule as phonemically different, in terms of some feature (phonetic or other), would also obscure the reason for its failure to change. This can better be handled by a special rule marking all proper nouns (not merely individual segments) with a special 'morpheme feature' which prevents the application of the general rule.

Two levels of representation can be meaningfully distinguished: the input representations of morphemes (and of morphs), and the phonetic output—frequently called the levels of systematic phonemics and systematic phonetics respectively. No evidence for any other significant phonological level, such as a taxonomic phonemic level, has been found. The systematic phonemic representation is in some ways more like the morphophonemic level of taxonomic phonemics, but cannot be identified with it. In this presentation the term 'phoneme' is used in the sense of systematic phoneme (unless qualified by 'taxonomic, traditional', etc.).

Morphemes are represented at the systematic phonemic level by a sequence of columns containing the distinctive feature specifications necessary for achieving the above aims; e.g., English *pin*, will have a phonemic form such as:

$$
\text{(a)}\quad
\begin{bmatrix} +\text{cns} \\ -\text{voc} \\ -\text{nas} \\ -\text{cnt} \\ +\text{grv} \\ +\text{dif} \\ -\text{vce} \end{bmatrix}
\begin{bmatrix} -\text{cns} \\ +\text{voc} \\ +\text{dif} \\ -\text{grv} \\ -\text{tns} \end{bmatrix}
\begin{bmatrix} +\text{cns} \\ -\text{voc} \\ +\text{nas} \\ -\text{grv} \end{bmatrix}
\quad \text{or}
$$

(b)

cns	+	−	+
voc	−	+	−
nas	−	0	+
cnt	−	0	0
grv	+	−	−
dif	+	+	0
tns	0	−	0
vce	−	0	0

These features, which must have plus or minus values, are generally called 'classificatory' features. Each column corresponds to a segment, although concern here is not with whole segments, but rather with the features within the segments. In (b) nondistinctive features are indicated by 'zero'. Morphemes as whole units may also possess markers of syntactic and other grammatical information in addition to morpheme features that mark them as irregular with regard to certain rules or as subject to certain special sets of rules.

At the systematic phonemic level utterances consist of morphemes and junctures. At the systematic phonetic level the utterances consist of sequences of feature columns (corresponding to the phones of a traditional segmental description), probably together with syllable boundaries and certain features, such as tone, that have the syllable as their domain (cf. Wang, 1967). But these feature matrices will differ from those at the phonemic level in two important respects; first, they will be fully specified for all classificatory features—not only those which are distinctive; e.g., the [n] of *pin* will contain the features [+diffuse, −flat, −continuant, −strident, +voiced, −tense, −sharp, −checked, etc.] as well; secondly, the features may have numerical values in addition to plus/minus values, e.g., the [ɪ] in *pin* will have received a stress value, depending upon its syntactic environment; e.g., [1 stress], [2 stress], or [3 stress].

The problem of specifying phonetic detail at the lowest level of the phonetic output has not been satisfactorily dealt with. One approach would be to add more binary features for those phonetic distinctions which cannot be stated in terms of the classificatory features (e.g., R. Wilson, 1966). Another approach would be to use numerical values; e.g., the labiodental : bilabial contrast might be expressed as [1 grave] : [2 grave].

One desirable result of the binary systematic phonemic approach is that a sharp line is drawn between redundant and distinctive features. Given a three-way phonemic contrast, say, p : t : s, five distinctive feature specifications are required to express the contrasts, for example,

	p	t	s
(a)			
cnt	—	—	+
grv	+	—	0

or

	p	t	s
(b) grv	+	—	—
cnt	0	—	+

In (a) graveness is redundant for /s/; in (b) continuance is redundant for /p/ (indicated by 'zero'). Consider now two approaches to the four-way system p : t : k : s:

	p	t	k	s
(c)				
grv	+	—	+	—
dif	+	0	—	0
cnt	0	—	0	+

or

	p	t	k	s
(d) grv	+	—	+	0
dif	+	+	—	0
cnt	0	0	0	+

In (c) /s/ contrasts with all other phonemes in terms of a specified plus or minus feature (i.e., with /k p/ in graveness, with /t/ in continuance). In (d), however, /s/ can be considered as contrasting with the stops only if a 'plus or minus' vs. 'zero' opposition is allowed. But if zero is allowed as a distinctive value, the distinction between redundant and distinctive information is lost here. System (c)'s eight distinctive features must be compared not only with the seven plus/minus features of (d), but with (d)'s five zero features as well—a total of twelve. For this reason, approach (d) is rejected, and only a strictly binary approach is allowed, that is, one limited to explicit plus and minus values.

EXERCISES

1. The taxonomic consonant phonemes of Walapai are listed as (Winter, 1966: 18): /p t r č k q ʔ v θ s š h m n ñ w l y/. Of /š/ we are told (19) that:

   'The status of /š/ is marginal at best. It was recorded repeatedly in the speech of female informants in the item /šáw/ *young*. This item has an alternant /θáw/ occurring in the speech of male informants, but not restricted to it. Closer investigation showed that š is a generalized baby-talk variant, limited, as far as could be detected, to the one item šaw. It does not seem advisable to assign š as a stylistically determined allophone to /θ/: a baby-talk utterance volunteered by a (male) informant showed two occurrences of š, one corresponding to normal /θ/, the other to /s/ ... .'

   (a) Discuss the desirability of including /š/ in the inventory of phonemes. Particularly consider the fact that a phoneme /š/ would require other phonemes—say, /θ/ and/or /s/—to be *distinctively* specified in one extra feature.

   (b) How could a field worker, his contact with Walapai limited, ascertain that /š/ occurs in 'baby-talk'? Under what conditions do you think the male informant volunteered the above data?

   (c) How might the formal description of Walapai best incorporate the information provided by the above nonformal, prose qualification of the phoneme inventory?

   (d) In a later discussion (20), the fricatives are given as: 'v θ s (š) h'. Does the use of parentheses adequately express the desired relationship here?

2. Another taxonomic study of Walapai gives the nasal phonemes as /m n ñ ŋ/ (Redden, 1966: 3). The phoneme /ŋ/ contrasts only with /ñ/, and in the single word /kíŋ/ *to ring* (as opposed to /kíñ/ 'YoSibling').

   (a) Do the data seem to support an independent /ŋ/ phoneme? How would the addition of an /ŋ/ affect the status of the other nasals?

   (b) How might [kíŋ] be fit into the Walapai phonological system without the recognition of an /ŋ/ phoneme that is independent in the same sense as /m n ñ/? (*Note*: [ŋ] should not be reinterpreted as a cluster.)

3. For most speakers of English, the morpheme 'you' has numerous phonetic manifestations, e.g., [yu, :] [yə], [ču :], [čə], etc. The morpheme *go* also corresponds to several phonetically different forms, as in [goʊ], [wɛnt], etc. Is the variation in form found with *you* different in nature from the variation in form with *go*? Which of the above data correspond to regular phonological processes active in Modern English?

4. A distinctive-feature analysis of Bengali obstruents and nasals shows (Ferguson and Chowdhury, 1960: 53):

	p	t	ṭ	c	k	b	d	ḍ	j	g	ph	th	ṭh	ch	kh	bh	dh	ḍh	jh	gh	s	m	n	ṅ
vocalic	−	−	−	−	−	−	−	−	−	−	−	−	−	−	−	−	−	−	−	−	−	+	+	+
consonantal	+	+	+	+	+	+	+	+	+	+	+	+	+	+	+	+	+	+	+	+	+	+	+	+
grave	+	−	±	−	+	+	−	±	−	+	+	−	±	−	+	+	−	±	−	+	○	+	−	+
compact	−	−	−	+	+	−	−	−	+	+	−	−	−	+	+	−	−	−	+	+	○	−	−	+
nasal	○	○	○	○	○	○	○	○	○	○	○	○	○	○	○	○	○	○	○	○	○	+	+	+
tense	−	−	−	−	−	−	−	−	−	−	+	+	+	+	+	+	+	+	+	+	○	○	○	○
voiced	−	−	−	−	−	+	+	+	+	+	−	−	−	−	−	+	+	+	+	+	−	○	○	○
discontinuous	○	○	○	○	○	○	○	○	○	○	○	○	○	○	○	○	○	○	○	○	−	○	○	○

The nasals are distinguished from the liquids, which are also '+vocalic, +consonantal,' by nasality; otherwise all the phonemes listed above are distinguished from those not listed in vocalicity or consonantality. The value '±' indicates a degree intermediate between 'plus' and 'minus'.

(a) How does the above use of features differ from the strictly binary approach of generative phonology? Do all phonemes contrast with all other phonemes solely in specified (i.e., other than '0') features?

(b) Restate the analysis in order to eliminate '±' values. The retroflex stops are nongrave. They can be described as 'flat' in contrast with the other obstruents. Be careful to use no more '+' or '−' specifications than are necessary in order to ensure a strictly binary system.

(c) In the above description is care exercised not to use '+' or '−' values with feature-specifications that can be considered redundant—i.e., that should have been left unspecified ('0')?

5. The following distinctive feature analysis has been proposed for Maori consonants (Hohepa 1967: 7):

	p	t	k	r	f	h	w	m	n	ŋ
consonantal	+	+	+	+	+	+	+	+	+	+
continuant	−	−	−	−	+	+	+	+	+	+
nasal	−	−	−	−	−	−	−	+	+	+
voiced	−	−	−	+	−	−	+	0	0	0
compact	−	−	+	0	−	+	0	−	−	+
grave	+	−	0	0	0	0	0	+	−	0

One way to test the strict binarity of such a classificatory matrix is to convert it to a tree diagram. List all phonemes at the top of the tree; then split them successively into groups of two on the basis of some feature for which all phonemes at any given node are specified as either plus or minus (i.e., all 'plus' phonemes in one group and all 'minus' phonemes in the other group). Each node can be developed independently of other nodes in the tree. When a node contains only one phoneme, the minimum binary feature specification for that phoneme has been attained in the given tree. If a matrix has not been set up on a strictly binary basis, such a tree will not be possible: at some node not all the phonemes will be specified plus or minus for some common feature, or a node with a single phoneme will have feature specifications not exploited in the branching tree diagram. If *all* phonemes of a node have the same value for some feature not yet exploited in the tree, then too many specifications have been made.

For example, corresponding to the following classificatory matrix, the tree A below can be constructed:

	p	t	k	m	n	r	l	?	h	i	a	u
vocalic	−	−	−	−	−	+	+	−	−	+	+	+
consonantal	+	+	+	+	+	+	+	−	−	−	−	−
obstruent	+	+	+	−	−							
grave	+	−	+	+	−					−	+	+
diffuse	+		−								−	+
continuant						−	+	−	+			

A

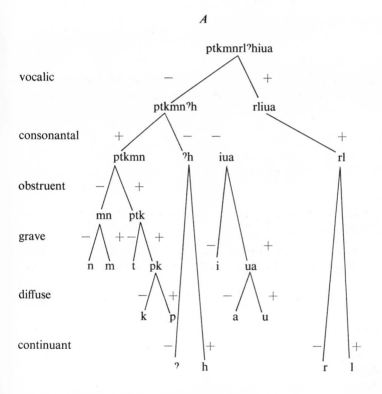

A more symmetrical tree will generally contain fewer specifications than one less symmetrical. Thus tree B, with 16 specifications, is more symmetrical than tree C, with 17.

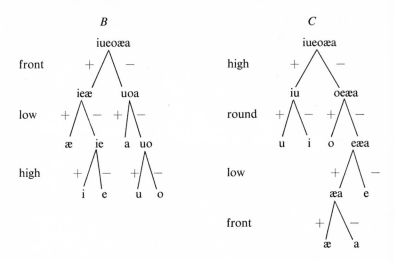

(a) Construct a tree diagram to check the strict binarity of the above Maori analysis, and evaluate the results. The vowels of Maori are represented as:

	i	e	u	o	a
consonantal	−	−	−	−	−
compact	−	±	−	±	+
grave	−	−	+	+	0

(b) Rewrite the vowel system to eliminate the '±' values. Replace 'compact' with 'high' and 'low'.

6. A study of Thai phonology presents the following classificatory feature representation of the consonants (Warotamasikkhadit, 1965: 14):

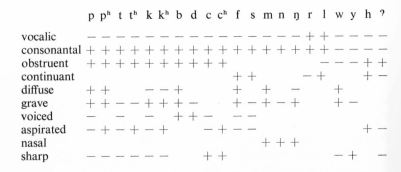

The author states (17) that 'the Jakobsonian binary distinctive features have been adopted. The information carried by a binary feature should be either a plus or a minus. A blank is not to be interpreted as a tertiary feature, but rather as a slot of either a plus or a minus feature specification.'

(a) Is the above approach one in which a blank need not be 'interpreted as a tertiary feature' and in which blanks are used to provide the optimal indication of feature redundancy? Where necessary, give any additional feature specifications required to preserve binarity; and, where possible, eliminate features that can be considered redundant.

(b) Have the phonemes in the Thai matrix been organized in a manner that allows one to check their binarity easily? What changes might be made?

CHAPTER 4

The Classificatory Features

The following list presents those classificatory features which have been in recent use. Revisions in the inventory of features and in the usage of older features have become commonplace during the past year, so that the list below can be safely said to represent usage only prior to the summer of 1967. In the discussion that follows, the illustrations of the features in given languages are based primarily upon actually proposed descriptions and should not be interpreted as prescriptive. Features that, in my opinion, can better be replaced by other features on the list (e.g., vocalic by syllabic) or whose acceptance seems questionable (e.g., peripheral) have been starred. A short abbreviation for most features follows in parenthesis. A second set of parentheses indicates the source of the feature (J = Jakobson, H = Halle, M = McCawley).

A. General (syllabicity-type) features:

      1. consonantal (cns) (J)
    *2. vocalic (voc) (J)
      3. obstruent (obs) (H)
      4. syllabic (syl) (M)

B. Oral-articulator features:

    *5. compact and diffuse (cmp; dif, dff) (J)
      6. grave and (*)acute (grv, act) (J)

    7. high and low   (M)
  *8. buccal   (buc)   (M)
  *9. high$_2$ (Kiparsky)
(*)10. mid   (Kiparsky)
 *11. low tonality   (H)
(*)12. peripheral   (prph)   (Stockwell)

C. Qualifying features:

    13. flat   (flt)   (J)
    14. sharp   (shp)   (J)
    15. retracted articulator   (retrac)   (M), or proximal   (prox)
        (Chomsky and Halle)

D. Manner features:

    16. continuant   (cnt)   (J)
    17. strident (strid, std)   (J)
    18. abrupt offset   (abrof)   (H)
    19. lateral   (lat)   (H)
    20. tense   (tns)   (J)

E. Nonoral-articulator features:

    21. voiced   (vce, voi)   (J)
    22. checked   (chk)   (J)
    23. nasal   (nas, nsl)   (J)

F. Prosodic features:

    24. long   (lng)
    25. stressed   (stress, str)
    26. accented   (acc)
    27. tone features: high pitch   (M)
                 high, echo   (Carrell)
                 contour, high, central, mid, falling, rising,
                 convex   (Wang)

A. The general (syllabicity-type) features are used to divide the inventory of systematic phonemes into the general classes: vowels, true consonants, glides (i.e., semivowels, and /h ?/), liquids and resonants.

'Consonantal' and 'vocalic' provide the four classes:

	true consonant (obstruent)	liquid (resonant)	glide	vowel
cns	+	+	−	−
voc	−	+	−	+

Russian is presented as (Halle, 1959):

	obstruents, nasals	/r l l'/	/y/	vowels
cns	+	+	−	−
voc	−	+	−	+

Combining the nasals and semivowels to give a general resonant class in Southern Paiute (which has no liquids) gives (Harms, 1966a):

	obstruents	nasals, /w y/	/h ʔ/	vowels
cns	+	+	−	−
voc	−	+	−	+

In Zanzibar Swahili (after Harris, 1951) the nasals and liquids can be grouped together:

	obstruents	nasals, liquids	/w y h/	vowels
cns	+	+	−	−
voc	−	+	−	+

A third general feature, 'obstruent', has been used recently, sometimes in place of 'vocalic' in the classificatory matrix. The three-class Finnish system is given as (McCawley, 1964):

	obstruents	nasals, liquids	vowels
cns	+	+	−
obs	+	−	

In this system vocalicity is, then, redundantly specified 'minus' for nasals and 'plus' for liquids in the morpheme structure rules. The only apparent motivation for the use of obstruence is that it makes it possible to establish a general resonant class and at the same time maintain Jakobson's original contrast of nasals and liquids in vocalicity (which is not done in the above Southern Paiute and Swahili examples).

All three features are used in the treatment of Japanese (McCawley, 1965):

	obstruents	nasals, liquid	/ʔ w y/	vowels
cns	+	+	−	−
voc			−	+
obs	+	−		

In Bolivian Quechua five general classes result:

	obstruents	nasals	liquids	/y w h/	vowels
obs	+	−	−	−	−
cns		+	+	−	−
voc		−	+	−	+

This represents the maximum number of possible general classes, since [+obstruent] will always be a subclass of the true consonants (i.e., [+cns, −voc]).

McCawley (1966) argues for a feature of syllabicity ([syl]) to replace vocalicity. This makes it possible to group the nasals and liquids more naturally than with Jakobson's vocalicity feature and provides a contrast between syllabic and nonsyllabic resonants (required in the treatment of languages such as Sanskrit). McCawley's most recent treatment of Finnish thus gives:

	obstruents	nasals, liquids	/w/	vowels
cns	+	+	−	−
syl			−	+
obs	+	−		

Note here the syllabicity alternation between [ü] (from [u] via vowel harmony) and [v] in Finnish [käü-dä] *to visit* and [käv-i] *visited.*

In assigning a given systematic phoneme to one of the above classes, the primary goal is to obtain the most general sets of natural classes with regard to the phonological rules. The notion of 'natural class' involves two considerations. First, it is a class of segments that can be specified with fewer features than any individual member of the class. To refer to the class of vowels in the Finnish system described above requires only the two features '−cns, +syl', whereas any given vowel requires several additional feature-specifications. Second, the features shared by the class members should be limited to those which have a certain degree of phonetic plausibility.

The difficulty of making clear-cut decisions concerning the phonetic plausibility of natural classes points up an area of current theory that needs to be further sharpened. Assignments can not be made on purely phonetic grounds. In Finnish, for example, certain generalizations can be adequately stated only if [h] is considered to arise from an underlying obstruent. In Southern Paiute, [r] is best assigned to the obstruent /t/. On the basis of rule function, Eugene Loos (1967) argues for treating nasals in Capanahua as continuant obstruents and for assigning the bilabial fricative /β/ to the class of resonants; thus:

	obstruents, nasals	/β r/	/y w ?/	vowels
cns	+	+	−	−
syl			−	+
obs	+	−		

Note also the above interpretation of Finnish /v/ as a glide.

The two universal classes of consonant and vowel (symbolized as 'C' and 'V') also are defined in terms of the general features. A consonant is any segment which is '+cns' or '−voc' (in Quechua, this might have to be expanded to include '+obs'); all other segments are vowels. It is not clear how the simplicity metric is to be applied to the symbols C and V, but it would seem reasonable to count them as fewer features than the two (or more) features required for the specification of particular general class types (e.g., C is more general than either of [+cns, −voc] or [−cns, −voc]). One argument in favor of the feature 'syllabic' is that once all consonants are specified for syllabicity, we can define all consonants as simply [−syl] and all vowels as [+syl].

B. The oral-articulator features subdivide classes of consonants and vowels with regard to primary area of articulation (which may be

further defined by the use of qualifying features; cf. C below). Jakobson's features compact/diffuse correspond to the two poles of the
articulatory dimensions:

    (a) for vowels: low/high
    (b) for consonants: back/front

Grave/acute correspond to:

    (a) for vowels: back/front
    (b) for consonants: peripheral/central

In standard practice either compact or diffuse (but not both) is used in
the description of consonants, but both are used with vowels; of
grave/acute only grave is used.

    Unlike the articulatory terms 'front', 'back', 'central', etc., these
features only denote relative frontness or backness, highness or lowness.
For example, the common four-vowel system /i e o a/ might be
analyzed as:

	i	e	o	a
grv	−	−	+	+
cmp	−	+	−	+

(Note that in other vowel systems /e/ normally would not be '+cmp'.)
The equally common five-vowel system, with an /u/ in addition to the
above vowels, as in Japanese, shows (McCawley, 1965):

	i	e	a	o	u
grv	−	−	+	+	+
dif	+	−	−	−	+
cmp			+	−	

The difference between central vowels and front vowels may also be
treated as a graveness contrast; e.g., for Komi the vowels /i e/ differ
from the central vowels /ɨ ə a/ and the back vowels /u o/ in graveness.
Most frequently back vowels are rounded (i.e., [+flat]), so that the
feature of flatness may be used instead of graveness to set them off.
Russian, which has the same five vowels as Japanese, is, nonetheless,
better described with flatness than with graveness, since in palatalized

environments all normally back vowels are fronted (i.e., reverse their graveness, which is nondistinctive). Thus:

	i	e	a	o	u
flt	−	−	−	+	+
dif	+	−	−	−	+
cmp		−	+		

An argument for the use of acuteness as well as graveness in the description of the Finnish vowels results in (Harms, 1966b):

	i	e	a	ä	u	ü	o	ö
act	+	+	−	−	−	−	−	−
cmp			+	+	−	−	−	−
dif	+	−			+	+	−	−
grv			+	−	+	−	+	−

The use of acute as well as grave here means that three points rather than two can be distinguished on the front-back scale (parallel to the use of compact and diffuse on the high-low scale). Acoustically, acuteness-graveness corresponds to the height of the second formant, and since the vowels /i e/ have higher second formants than /ü ö ä/, they can be set off by acuteness. /ü ö ä/, in turn, have higher second formants than /u o a/, which can then be distinguished by graveness. This results in a natural break between the traditional Finnish neutral vowels /i e/ and those vowels which undergo vowel harmony (according to which the nonacute vowels must agree in graveness).

The two sets of features provide for four series of consonants, e.g.:

	p	t	č	k	(as in English or Russian)
dif	+	+	−	−	
grv	+	−	−	+	

or

	p	t	k	q	(as in South Greenlandic Eskimo)
dif	+	+	−	−	
grv	+	−	−	+	

Again note the relative use of graveness with the compact (i.e., [−dif]) consonants. If more than four series of consonants are present, other features must be used (see below).

Recently, strong arguments have been advanced for a new feature 'high', which completely replaces diffuseness (McCawley, 1967). In articulatory terms, highness gives:

(a) for vowels: high vowels are [+high]
                  mid and low vowels are [−high]
(b) for consonants: labials, dentals, and alveolars are [−high]
                      postalveolar to uvular consonants are [+high]

This means that the above illustrations would be restated so that: (a) for vowels 'dif' is replaced with 'high' without changing the plus/minus values; (b) for consonants '+dif' is replaced by '−high'; '−dif', by '+high'. One important implication of this new feature is that the common change [ty] > [č] can be seen as assimilation ([t] is '−high', [y] and [č] are '+high'), whereas with diffuseness it must be treated as some kind of dissimilation (since [t] and [y] are '+dif', but [č] is '−dif'). This now parallels the equally common assimilation [k] > [č] before [y], often with fusion, and front vowels, where [č] and [k] differ in graveness, and [č], [y] and front vowels are nongrave. Both these instances of assimilation support the notion of common features for consonants and vowels.

Earlier, McCawley (1966) had proposed a feature 'buccal', which functioned in the same manner as 'high', except that '+buc' = '−high' and '−buc' = '+high'.

Since the feature 'high' leaves 'compact' restricted to use solely with vowels, McCawley (1967) here suggests a second articulatory-based feature 'low' (such that '+low' = '+cmp' and '−low' = '−cmp').

Paul Kiparsky (1967b) also uses a feature 'high', differing from McCawley's 'high' in being limited to use with vowels. He further argues for a feature 'mid', which, together with 'high', replaces earlier 'diffuse' and 'compact', in describing a Swiss German dialect reputed to have four distinctive degrees of tongue height with front vowels, thus:

	æ	ɛ	e	i
high	−	−	+	+
mid	−	+	+	−

In place of graveness, Halle uses a feature of 'low tonality' in his description of Russian (1959), which incorporates the properties of both graveness and flatness (apparently following the suggestion in Jakobson, Fant, and Halle, 33–34); thus giving:

	labials	dentals	palatals	velars	i	u	e	o	a
diffuse					+	+	−	−	−
compact	−	−	+	+			−	−	+
low tonality	+	−	−	+	−	+	−	+	

Stockwell has proposed a feature 'peripheral' (1966) to set off central vowels from front and back vowels. This may be desirable in four-vowel Cashibo, which recognizes a natural class /i u/ as opposed to /ɨ/, since /i u/ in terms of graveness or flatness will share no feature which /ɨ/ does not also possess. Thus:

	i	u	ɨ	a
periph	+	+	−	−
flat	−	+		
high			+	−

Harms (1967) also argues for the use of peripheralness in the development of the Permic languages. The Eastern Vyčegda dialect of Komi has the central (grave) rounded vowels /ɯ ȯ/ in opposition to the back (peripheral) rounded vowels /u o/—a system which can not be easily described without the feature 'peripheral':

	i	ɯ	u	e	ȯ	o	a
high	+	+	+	−	−	−	−
low				−	−	−	+
prph	+	−	+	+	−	+	
flt	−	+	−		+		

The high degree of dialectal variation in the rounding of central vowels in Komi and Udmurt weighs against distinctive flatness, even where the typical Permic system of /i ɨ u e ə o a/ can be handled with flatness and graveness. Proto-Udmurt */i ɨ u o/ must have shifted at an early stage to */i ɨ ɯ u/ respectively. This was followed in Besermyan by a merger of */ɯ/ with */u/ and of */ə/ with */e/, which can be explained as a single rule making these central vowels peripheral.

One difficulty with peripheralness is that it allows phonemic systems with three vowel phonemes of the same tongue height that agree in rounding—say */i ü ɯ u/. With flatness and graveness as the sole tonality features, the generally accepted hypothesis that such systems will not be found results directly from the universal phonetic system. The addition of peripheralness requires an *ad hoc* constraint that peripheralness and graveness cannot both be distinctive in the same system (although the graveness of vowels must be redundantly specified in the case that peripheralness is distinctive—e.g., in the case of the high nonperipheral flat vowels [ü] and [ɯ]).

The glides /y w/ normally will agree with the vowels /i u/ respectively, except for syllabicity (or vocalicity). Most frequently they will contrast distinctively in graveness. How to contrast /h/ and /ʔ/ with the semivowels is problematical. In Quechua the glides are broken down in the following manner:

	y	w	h
dif	+	+	−
grv	−	+	

but other features, such as voice, may be used. /ʔ/ is often 'minus' for all features. /h/, on the other hand, could be handled in various ways at the phonemic level, but in its phonetic realization it will take the same positional features (i.e., grave, high (or diffuse), flat) as the nearest vowel in the same syllable.

C. The qualifying features 'flat' and 'sharp' indicate the effect of a secondary articulation that has the effect of attenuating or augmenting the tonality (graveness or acuteness) of the primary articulation. These features must be thought of as musical (acoustic) terms rather than as geometrical terms. Flatting, then, is a lowering, and sharping a raising of the tonality feature (generally reflected in the height of the second formant on a spectrogram).

Flatness is produced by a secondary articulation that increases the volume of the oral cavity; e.g., lip rounding or pharyngealization. Thus the Indo-European velar consonants k : kʷ are opposed in flatness; that is,

	p	t	k′	k	kʷ
high	−	−	−	+	+
grv	+	−	−	+	+
flt				−	+

Note, however, the five-series Southern Paiute system (Harms, 1966a):

	p	t	č	k	kʷ
cmp	−	−	+	+	+
grv	+	−	−	−	+
strid			+	−	

Since stridence has been used to contrast č : k, only one tonality feature (graveness) is needed (cf. Halle's use of low tonality in Russian) although this practice is questionable.

Retroflex consonants are treated as flat (as opposed to 'plain' consonants). In many languages /r/ also produces flatting (noticeable in the effect upon surrounding vowels or its relationship to the semivowel /w/, so that it would seem plausible to contrast r : l in terms of flatness (or perhaps graveness), if the more usual continuance opposition is not feasible, as in English.

The so-called emphatic consonants of Arabic are treated as flat (Jakobson, 1957), although this has recently been challenged (McCawley, 1967).

Ingressive /ɓ kp/ in Igbo are treated as flat (Carrell, 1966), but the interpretation here is not clear, since only labial or coarticulated stops are involved and no /ɗ/ occurs in the dialect studied. (See also tenseness below.)

Flat has been used to handle relative degrees of graveness, as in the velar : uvular contrast in the five-position Quechua system.

	p	t	č	k	q
dif	+	+	−	−	−
grv	+	−	−	+	+
flt				−	+

With vowels flatness simply refers to rounding. An earlier treatment of Finnish (Halle, 1964) gives:

	i	e	a	ä	u	ü	o	ö
flt	−	−	−	−	+	+	+	+
cmp	−	−	+	+				
dif	+	−			+	+	−	−
grv			+	−	+	−	+	−

Cf. also the Russian system with distinctive flatness illustrated in B above.) Turkish has the system:

	i	i̇	ü	u	e	a	ö	o
high	+	+	+	+	−	−	−	−
flt	−	−	+	+	−	−	+	+
grv	−	+	−	+	−	+	−	+

Sharpness is used primarily for palatalized consonants, as in Russian. But note the use of sharp and flat in the analysis of the Japanese glides (McCawley, 1965):

	ʔ	w	y
shp	−	−	+
flt	−	+	

A new feature, 'retracted articulation', has been proposed by McCawley (1966) to account for the following types of contrasts: (a) bilabial : labiodental, (b) interdental : dental, (c) dental : alveolar, (d) apico-palatal : dorso-palatal, (e) velar : uvular. This is essentially the same as the feature 'proximal' posited by Chomsky and Halle (to appear).

In the above Quechua five-position system k : q would be contrasted by the use of this feature instead of flatness. (See also D(b) below).

D. The following features are correlated primarily with the manner of articulation.

(a) Continuant (vs. interrupted) opposes stops and affricates to other consonants, r : l, ʔ : h. The nasal (stop) consonants m, n, ŋ, etc. are normally seen as phonetically noncontinuant, thus allowing for nasalized (continuant) fricatives as well.

In Southern Paiute the oppositions č : š, ʔ : h are based upon continuance (but k : (č/š) is based upon stridence). Finnish t : s and Hindi c : s are also treated as continuance oppositions. In Hindi, with only one continuant obstruent and stops that must be distinctively marked for both voicing and aspiration (tenseness), two approaches are possible:

	/s/	all other obstruents
(1) cnt	+	−

	p	t	ṭ	s	c	k	voiceless aspirated	voiced plain	voiced aspirated
vce	−	−	−	−	−	−	−	+	+
tense	−	−	−	−	−	−	+	−	+
(2) high	−	−	−	+	+	+			
grv	+	−	−	−	−	+			
flt		−	+						
cnt				+	−				

The two approaches give different natural classes of obstruents (e.g., only in (2) is /s c/ a natural class). In (1) all obstruents must be distinctively specified for continuance (although /s/ need only be specified as '+cnt'), whereas in (2) only /c/ and /s/ need be specified (although /s/ here requires specification for voicing, tenseness, highness, and graveness as well). Assuming that /s/ is not overwhelmingly frequent in the spellings of morphemes, (2) would represent a substantial lexical savings (cf. Chapter 8). It should be noted, however, that once redundant features are specified, /s c/ constitute a natural class in (1) as well.

The λ : 1 contrast in Classical Nahuatl should also be treated as a continuance contrast.

(b) Strident (vs. mellow) opposes fricatives (plus) to nonfricatives; affricates (plus) to stops; labiodental, dental, and uvular (plus) to bilabial, interdental, and velar fricatives. Thus, ř : r (Czech), c : t) Russian), č : k (Southern Paiute), v : β (Ewe), s : θ (Eng.), x : χ (Circassian). Homorganic stops and affricates are generally opposed in stridence, but normally stop vs, fricative contrasts will be handled with continuance (as Finnish t : s). 'Retracted articulation' (cf. C above) would replace stridence in such contrasts as v : β, s : θ, t^s : $t^θ$, x : χ. 'Abrupt offset' would replace it in affricate : stop contrasts (cf. D(c) below).

(c) 'Abrupt offset', or 'abrupt release', has been proposed by Halle to contrast stops with affricates (in place of stridence; cf. McCawley, 1966, 1967). This is essential in Chipewyan, which has a three-way t : $t^θ$: t^s contrast (where the [−abrof] $t^θ$ and t^s would be handled in turn by retracted articulation or stridence). McCawley suggests the following use of this feature (1966):

	stops	affricates	flaps & trills
cnt	−	−	+
abrof	+	−	+

(d) 'Lateral' is used to distinguish laterally released stops and lateral fricatives (ł) from the corresponding apical obstruents in various Amerindian languages. For example, Chipewyan's eight consonant series may be analyzed as:

	b	d	λ	dᵟ	ʒ	ǯ	g	gʷ
high	−	−	−	−	−	+	+	+
grv	+	−	−	−	−	−	+	+
abrof		+	−	−	−			
lat			+	−	−			
retrac				−	+			
flt							−	+

Chipweyan's /ł l/ also fit into the obstruent continuant series with the same four features as for /λ/ and are opposed in voicing.

(e) The opposition tense (vs. lax) is used to handle a wide range of phenomena:

1. Long (vs. short) with both consonants and vowels; e.g., vowel length in Latin, r̄ : r in Spanish. In English, the systematic vowel phonemes contrast in tenseness, and the realizations of the tense vowels are either long or diphthongized (Chomsky and Halle, to appear); for example, /i/ > [ɪ], /ī/ > [ay], /e/ > [ɛ], /ē/ > [i :], /æ/ > [æ], /ǣ/ > [ey], etc. In the description of Alsatian German (Becker, 1967), however, both tenseness and length must be used as independent features (where tenseness indicates a closer (vs. more open) vowel quality).

2. Aspirated consonants (as in Hindi).

3. Fortis (vs. lenis) articulation of consonants. In Danish, in certain positions [t] : [d] contrast in voicing and in relative tenseness; in other positions [d] : [ð] contrast in continuance and relative tenseness. In this second environment, the phoneme /t/, defined as (relatively more) tense, is realized as [d]; the (relatively more) lax phoneme /d/, as [ð]. At the phonetic level, however, all [d]'s have the same feature-specification (cf. Jakobson, Fant, and Halle, 1951 : 5–6).

4. Certain qualitative vowel contrasts related to a retraction of the body of the tongue (Ladefoged, 1964: 38–40), especially in the description of African languages with a tense-lax vowel harmony. For example, in Igbo four pairs of vowels are opposed in tenseness (Carrell, 1966; with the tense vowel to the left): i : e, ɛ : a, u : ɵ, o : ɔ (where [ɵ] is a lax midrounded vowel).

5. Close (vs. open) vowel articulation; e.g., German [i] : [ɪ], [e] : [ɛ], etc.

Tenseness would seem to be a convenient feature for contrasting [ə] (lax) to so-called 'full vowels'. The appropriateness of the description of French vowel contrasts in terms of tenseness (cf. Jakobson, Fant, and Halle, 1951) has recently been challenged (Rohrer, 1967). Perhaps tenseness can be used to handle implosive stops in various African languages.

E. The nonoral-articulator features are: voiced, nasal, and checked. The first two correspond to the conventional articulatory usage of voicing and nasalization. Checked is used for glottalization; i.e., ejectives, coarticulated segments and sequences of phonologically bound glottal catch plus preceding or following segment. Systematic vowel phonemes that contrast in voicing have been posited for Southern Paiute (Harms, 1966a). The nasal contrast is not known to occur with vowels at the phonemic level. In the systematic phonemic analyses of languages with nasal vowels (such as French, Igbo), the interpretation of these as vowel plus nasal consonant has consistently proved superior to the unit nasal vowel solution (cf. Rohrer, 1967, Carrell, 1966).

F. Numerous prosodic features are found:

(a) 'Long' is used to handle contrasts which are primarily quantitative, such as the Hungarian vowel system. Long consonant phonemes have been posited for Faroese (O'Neil, 1964). The traditional contrast between long consonants and geminate clusters is probably unrealistic. If, instead, a convention were adopted which allowed any sequence of two identical consonants to satisfy the structural description of a long consonant and any long consonant to satisfy the structural description of two consonants (say, for indicating closed syllables), then in the description of languages such as Finnish and Estonian, both lexical and rule advantages (such as in the treatment of consonant gradation, which must apply to lexically long stops as well as to geminate stops formed across morpheme boundary) would result. (See also 'tenseness' above.)

(b) Only a single stress feature 'stressed' (sometimes also 'accented') has been proposed. This means that at the systematic phonemic level a single plus/minus distinction has sufficed to account for the various phonetic realizations of stress. For example, in English up to five relative degrees of stress are derived from underlying morpheme representations that do not require any specification of stress (Chomsky and Halle, to appear). (These relative degrees of stress are stated in n-ary terms; e.g., [1-stress], [4-stress], etc.). Halle uses 'accented' in Russian (1959) to represent stress (cf. 'stressed' in Cherry, Halle, and Jakobson, 1953).

(c) 'Accented' is found instead of 'stressed' and also in the description of a tonal-type accent, as in Japanese (McCawley, 1965). In Japanese only one 'accented' feature is needed in order to account for the accent and pitch phenomena.

(d) A wide array of tone features has been used; e.g., 'high pitch' for Serbo-Croatian tonal accent (McCawley, 1963; also Browne and McCawley, 1965); 'high' and 'echo' tone features are used in the description of the terrace-tone system of Igbo—although only high tone is distinctive at the phonemic level (i.e., vowels must be marked '+high' or '−high', but echo tone values are provided by rules that use syntactic and phonological information). The tonal 'high' must be kept distinct from the oral-articulatory 'high'. Perhaps such accentual features should be capitalized—'HIGH'.

In the first published attempt to systematize the treatment of tone within a generative framework, W. S-Y Wang (1967) proposes a system of seven binary tone features (i.e., contour, high, central, mid, rising, falling, and convex). Wang considers tone features to occur with the syllable as a whole rather than with individual segments (but does not show how the system would work; cf. Chapter 10 below for a discussion of the syllable). The tones of Amoy Hokkien are given as:

	Ia	Ib	II	IIIa	IIIb	IVa	IVb
	˥	˦	˥˨	˥˩	˦	˩	˥
long	+	+	+	+	+	−	−
high	+	+	+	−	−	−	+
falling	−	−	+	+	−	(+)	(−)
rising	−	+	(−)	(−)	(−)	(−)	(−)

(I have taken the liberty of designating the features in parentheses as redundant, although perhaps a different breakdown into distinctive and redundant features would be desirable. It is not clear from Wang's treatment, whether the feature 'long' is also considered to belong to the syllable level.)

The general lack of agreement on the basic set of features and on the use of particular features, even within the Jakobsonian framework, points up serious problems which remain to be dealt with. One goal is to obtain a single universal set of features, capable of adequately representing the phonological generalizations of all languages in a natural, direct manner. The basic set of features can be viewed as a hypothesis about language, subject to empirical validation. Arguments for adding new features to the list or for altering the basic features must demonstrate the inadequacy of the basic hypothesis. Such arguments, however, cannot be based upon an appeal to the simplicity metric, for the features themselves are elements in the simplicity metric. Phonemic solutions that do not assume the same set of features cannot be compared in terms of simplicity. The claim must be that one solution provides a more reasonable hypothesis of the phonological structure of the language in question. A second, equally important goal is to sharpen the definitions of the individual features. Only to the extent that the physical properties and functional constraints on each feature are clearly stated can strong claims be made for any given set of features.

EXERCISES

1. In each of the following groups of sounds, eliminate *one* sound which does not fit as well as the others. State the basis for your decision (in articulatory and/or distinctive feature terms).
   (a) [i ö ü a]
   (b) [p ɸ m f β̃]
   (c) [p k e u a]
   (d) [č t k x š]
   (e) [ʒ ž y e u w g]
   (f) [kʷ t̪ u gb ɓ p]

2. The following statements provide evidence for and against various distinctive features and their functions. Determine what features are involved and the relevance of the evidence (or argument) to the use or inclusion in the systematic phonetic system of the features in question.

(a) Diola-Fogny has the five tense vowels /i̠ e ə o u̠/ and five lax vowels /i ɛ a ɔ u/ and a vowel harmony rule which tenses any lax vowel to the corresponding tense vowel if a tense vowel occurs in the same word. /ə/, the tense counterpart of /a/, is described as an 'unrounded high-midcentral vowel [under stress]; otherwise it takes a slightly lower position which is similar to the English schwa' (Sapir, 1965: 6, 11).

(b) Diola-Fogny also has distinctive vowel length, which, in effect, doubles the number of vowel phonemes (cf. (a) above).

(c) Atsugewi [n] contrasts with both [m] and [ŋ]. We are told that '/m/ and /ŋ/ are not in contrast in my material, /ŋ/ occurring only before /k/ and /m/ never there, but it would be casuistry to attempt to define a nasal phoneme which would include them but exclude /n/: (non-alveolar?) with [ŋ] between them....' (Olmsted, 1958: 218).

(d) The description of certain English dialects leads to the statements (Sledd, 1966: 29): '... both !1!s next optionally vocalize ... before labials and !k! (not !g!)' and (footnote to the preceding) 'there is no final !g!, and syllable-break hinders the vocalization. In a more precise statement, !g! might not need to be excepted.'

(e) In Kolokuma Ijo, vowels and /w r y/ (but not /l/) are nasalized in the same syllable as a nasal. '/r/ is usually a single flap, but is apparently fricative for at least some speakers' (Williamson, 1965: 20).

(f) The Gokana dialect of Ogoni is said to have, in addition to the nasal consonants /m n/, a phoneme /M/ described as a nasal resonant'. 'In initial position in the word M is realized as a tone-bearing, voiced, nasal contoid homorganic with the allophone of the following consonant. (M does not occur in word-initial position before a vowel.) .... Doubled and in all other positions, M is realized as a tone-bearing, voiced, bilabial nasal ....' Examples:

/mɛ̃n/	[mɛ̃n]	'neck' ([ˈ] is midtone.)
/nɔ̃m/	[nɔ̃m]	*animal*
/nɔ̃M/	[nɔ̃m̃]	*imitated me*
/Ḿnɔ̃m/	[ńnɔ̃m]	*bird*
/Ḿkɛ̃m/	[ŋ́kɛ̃m]	*small*
/MM̀/	[m̄m̀]	*in*

The glottal catch in Ogoni is described with reference to boundaries which occur 'between two V or between V and M' (Brosnahan, 1964: 45).

(g) In Tillamook 'there are postvelars which are best described as having a kind of [ɔ] timbre, apparently created by cupping of the tongue, not by any rounding of the lips. Similarly, there are front velars with [i] coloring, and again the effect is created entirely inside the mouth ....

Tillamook /w/ also involves this sort of internal rounding, so that it inaccurate to characterize it as a labial element at all' (Thompson an Thompson, 1966: 316). Note further that these velars are opposed t plain velars, giving /k kʷ q qʷ/, etc. Other voiceless stops are /t c č

(h) In Arabela, /a/ is realized as [æ] after /š y/ or after /i e/ (perhap separated by a single C or Cw) (Rich, 1963: 198). (See below for th phonemes of Arabela.)

(i) In Southern Paiute, root initial /ŋʷ/ is realized as [m] or |w| in wor initial position (Harms, 1966a: 228).

(j) Maru requires a rule that inserts the stops /t/ and /k/ following wor ending in a high front vowel or a high back vowel respectively (c Burling, 1966). The only final stops are [p t k ʔ].

(k) In Cocama, /ð/ is realized as [y] before [i] (Faust and Pike, 195⁹ 18).

(l) The consonants of Araucanian are given as: /p t̠ t č k β ð s γ m n ñ ŋ 1̠ l l' r w y/ (where /t̠ ð n̠ 1̠/ are dental or interdental an /t n l/ are alveolar) (Suárez, 1959: 178–89; cf. also Echeverría an Contreras, 1965).

(m) In Maxakalí, a vowel is added after a word-final stop, and the stop optionally deleted. After [p], an [o] is added; after [t], [a]; after [č], [i after [k], [ɨ] (McCawley, 1967).

(n) Quechua high vowels /i u/ are lowered to [e o] in the environment c uvular obstruents of (the five obstruent series /p t č k q/, etc.).

(o) Cocama '[w, β, v] are freely fluctuating allophones of /w/ occurrin before /i/ and /ü/. [f], occurring only preceding [ř], is in complementar distribution with [w]' (Faust and Pike, 1959: 16). The other phoneme are /ɨ u a p t c č k s š m n r l w ð h/.

(p) Nootka has the consonant phonemes, among others, /p pʔ m mʔ t t n nʔ c cʔ s λ λʔ ł/ (the remaining consonants being glides or com pact voiceless obstruents). In English loanwords in Nootka, Englis /r l/ are often replaced by /n/ : *table* > /ti · pin/, *apples* > he · pinis, *rice* > /na · yis/; English /b v/, by /m/ : *bit* > /mi · t/, *Victoria* > /mito · ni/ (Mattingly, 1960: 80–81).

3. The feature illustrations in Chapter 4 show very little agreement in the us of the features. Restate the exemplified systems and subsystems in terms c the nonstarred features on the list and restrict their phonetic values a much as possible.

4. Construct feature matrices for the following systems:

(a) Cayuvava (Key, 1961): /p t č k b d ʒ β s š h m n ñ r i e æ ɨ u o ɔ/.

(b) Arabela (Rich, 1963): /p t k s š m n h w y i e a o u/. /h/ is nasalized and causes following vowels to become nasalized.

(c) Wichita (Garvin, 1950): /t k kʷ c s w r h ʔ i i· e e· u u· a a·/. /kʷ/ is coarticulated or followed by a labial release. /r/ has nasalized allophones initially, before /t c/ and before or after /r/.

(d) Logba (Ladefoged, 1964: 54): /p t c k' k kp b d ʒ ḍ g' g gb m n ñ ŋ ɸ f š s x β v ẓ ž h/. /ḍ ẓ/ are retroflex. /kp gb/ are coarticulated.

(e) Tillamook (Thompson and Thompson, 1966): /t c č k q kʷ qʷ tʔ cʔ ƛʔ čʔ kʔ qʔ kʔʷ qʔʷ s ɬ š x x̣ xʷ x̣ʷ n l y w ʔ h i e ə a/. '/ƛʔ/ has an allophone [λ] which occurs only in reduplicative prefixes to bases beginning in /ƛʔ/' (314).

CHAPTER 5

Phonological Rules

Phonological feature rules often take a form such as

(i) $$\begin{bmatrix} aF_1 \\ bF_2 \end{bmatrix} \longrightarrow [cF_3]$$

where F*i* indicates given features, and the letters a, b, c, indicate eithe
a given 'plus' or 'minus' value, for example,

(ii) $$\begin{bmatrix} -high \\ -flt \end{bmatrix} \longrightarrow [-grv]$$

The square brackets indicate a single phoneme or phone segment. The
features within the brackets to the left of the arrow indicate the struc
tural description that must be satisfied for the given rule to apply; fo
example, Rule (i) will apply to any segment that contains the feature:
'aF$_1$' and 'bF$_2$'; Rule (ii), to any segment which is nonhigh and nonflat
The segment in question will normally contain other features as well
but the rule refers only to those features which are immediately relevan
to the situation expressed in the rule; thus [e], [a], and [ə] contain the
features '−high, −flt' (plus other features not relevant here), so that
the Rule (ii) would apply to each of these three phones.

The brackets to the right of the arrow indicate the value(s) that any
features specified there must receive within the segments that meet the
structural description. For example, Rule (i) specifies that any segment
that contains aF$_1$ and bF$_2$ will have a value of 'c' for feature F$_3$; Rule
(ii) states that any phone that is 'nonhigh' and 'nonflat' must also be
'nongrave'.

The structural description for a rule may involve an environment in addition to the features of the segment to the left of the arrow:

(iii) $\begin{bmatrix} +\text{voc} \\ -\text{cns} \end{bmatrix}$ $\longrightarrow$ [$-$grv]   in evironment $\begin{bmatrix} +\text{cns} \\ +\text{shp} \end{bmatrix}$ __

i.e., vowels are nongrave (front) immediately following a sharp (palatalized) consonant. The words 'in the environment' are commonly replaced by the slash '/':

(iv)   [$+$obs] $\longrightarrow$ [$-$vce] / —$\ddagger$

i.e., word-final obstruents are voiceless. In fact, all of the Rules (i)–(iv) are context sensitive (i.e., require an environment). In (i, ii) the environment is entirely within the segment affected by the rule; e.g., (ii) could also be stated as:

(v)   [   ] $\longrightarrow$ [$-$grv] / $\begin{bmatrix} \underline{} \\ -\text{high} \\ -\text{flt} \end{bmatrix}$

where the empty segment brackets mean 'any segment'. Thus (v) may be read: any segment that contains the features '$-$high, $-$flt' (indicated by placing the environment bar within the segment) must be '$-$grv'. The following rule is context free:

(vi)   [   ] $\longrightarrow$ [$-$tns]

i.e., any segment is nontense (lax).

These rules contrast with rules of the type

(vii)   a $\longrightarrow$ æ

in several important respects. First, unlike Rule (vii), the features immediately to the right of the arrow do not replace the features to the left of the arrow (e.g., the segments resulting from Rule (ii) will contain, among others, the features '$+$buc, $-$flt, $-$grv ... ').

Secondly, within the generative approach rules are often best considered as constraints upon given segment types and sequences of segments, rather than as devices for producing changes in the segments. Consider the situation in which one segment already has the features '$-$high, $-$flt, $-$grv ... ' before the application of Rule (ii), whereas a second segment has the features '$-$high, $-$flt, $+$grv ... '. The rule applies to both segments, but only in the second segment will a change result. The primary concern is that the rules express as directly as possible the phonological generalizations of the language.

Feature rules can be used to specify features that were previously unspecified, or to switch the plus or minus values already specified; thus Rule (ii) above could be used to add a graveness specification 'minus' to a segment in which graveness was redundant and had not yet been assigned a plus or minus value. Segments may be added or deleted; thus:

$$\text{(viii)} \qquad \text{null} \longrightarrow \begin{bmatrix} +\text{voc} \\ -\text{cns} \\ +\text{high} \\ -\text{flt} \end{bmatrix} / \text{ C\_\_C}$$

i.e., between two consonants an [i] is inserted; or

$$\text{(ix)} \qquad [+\text{obs}] \longrightarrow \text{null} / \ddagger\_\_ [+\text{obs}]$$

i.e., if two obstruents occur initially, the first one is deleted. (Instead of 'null', the symbol 'Ø' is sometimes used.) Features cannot be deleted from within a segment; nor could this ever be desirable, for reasons which should be obvious in light of the distinctiveness criterion discussed below.

The distinctiveness criterion is a condition imposed upon rules to guarantee a rigorously binary system. According to this condition no rule is well-formed (acceptable) that exploits a contrast between specified ('+' or '−'), and unspecified ('0'), features. In effect, for all segments possibly relevant to the structural description of a given rule, there must be a way of determining solely on the basis of 'plus' and 'minus' feature values whether or not the rule is to apply. Consider, for example, the following five-vowel system at a stage before any redundant features have been specified:

	i	u	e	o	a
high	+	+	−	−	−
low	0	0	−	−	+
flt	−	+	−	+	0
grv	0	0	0	0	0

The distinctiveness criterion would reject Rule (ii) at this stage as improperly formulated, because /a/, which is nonhigh, has not yet been specified for flatness. Given the desirability of applying Rule (ii) here, two paths are open:

1. Additional features may be added to the structural description of (ii) that unambiguously include or exclude /a/; thus

$$
\text{(ii')} \qquad \begin{bmatrix} -\text{high} \\ -\text{low} \\ -\text{flt} \end{bmatrix} \longrightarrow [-\text{grv}]
$$

i.e., (a) we would then know the highness value for all vowels; (b) of those vowels which are nonhigh, the compactness value is specified; (c) for nonhigh, noncompact vowels, the flatness value is specified.
2. A rule could be inserted prior to (ii) that will specify /a/'s flatness value, e.g.,

$$
\text{(pre-ii)} \qquad \begin{bmatrix} -\text{high} \\ +\text{low} \end{bmatrix} \longrightarrow [-\text{flt}]
$$

It may be further noted that even if we ignore the distinctiveness criterion, Rule (ii) could not apply to the above system without assigning an interpretation to the '0flt' value of /a/: 1. The rule could be seen as applying to /a/, since it does not contrast explicitly with the structural description; or 2. The rule could be seen as inapplicable, since /a/ does not exactly fit the structural description. Thus two conflicting results could be obtained, both of which require assigning some value to the '0' (cf. Lightner, 1963a).

The distinctiveness criterion thus requires that each phoneme contrast with every other phoneme in at least one specified feature. If this were not the case, no rules could be given for filling redundant feature values. Consider the nondistinctive (improper) analysis of the three vowel system:

	i	u	a
high	+	+	0
low	0	0	+

No rules can be devised to fill in the zeros without abandoning the distinctiveness criterion, since we cannot identify either the high vowels or the low vowel without contrasting specified feature values with '0'.

EXERCISES

1. Write rules that specify the redundant features for the feature matrixes that you prepared as solutions for Exercise 4(a–e) of Chapter 4. (As a class assignment, one common matrix for each system should be selected.) Be careful not to alter distinctively specified features, since a contrast will be irretrievably lost. Note that although rules do not operate upon phonemic feature charts rules such as these are required to specify redundant features in individual segments within morphemes. Do not worry about rule abbreviations until you have read Chapter 7, but note situations where abbreviation would seem desirable. Order your rules for maximum economy.

2. Restate as rules the following statements given in Exercise 2 of Chapter 4. Consider all redundant features to be specified.

   (c): Atsugewi nasals.

   (d): English /l/. Consider the rule to apply to any English [l]-sound.

   (h): Arabela /a/.

   (i): Southern Paiute /ŋʷ/. Consider the [ŋʷ] that gives initial [w] to be a cluster and the [ŋʷ] that gives initial [m] to be a unit phoneme. Initial clusters are not permitted in Southern Paiute.

   (k): Cocama /ð/.

   (o): Cocama /w/ allophones. The phonemes of Cocama are /i ü ɨ u a p t c č w ð s š m n l r h/. To indicate free variation, mark the rule as 'optional'.

3. (a) Give the Walapai rule for the baby-talk [ś] articulation of underlying /s/ and /θ/ (cf. Chapter 3, Exercise 1).

   (b) Give the rule that determines the short noncompact vowel allophones in Atsugewi (cf. Chapter 2, Exercise 2). Assume /ʔ/ to be the only glide.

4. Write rules to handle the following phenomena:

   (a) In Arabela, a consonant between two stressed vowels is lengthened; e.g., /'po'konaki/ > ['po'k·onāγiʔ] (Rich, 1963).

   (b) In certain Estonian dialects, /l/ is palatalized following /i ü/ (other vowels are /u e ö ə o ä a/) before a labial consonant, e.g. [kül'm] *cold*, [il'm] *weather*.

   (c) Finnish intervocalic short /t/ is lost between two unstressed vowels, e.g., /talota/ > [táloa] *house* (partitive).

   (d) Upper Chehalis has four vowels /e o ə a/, long and short. Underlying /ə a/ are both realized as [a] when not stressed (Kinkade, 1966).

   (e) In Diola-Fogny, /k k'/ are both realized as [k']:

1. for certain speakers, before high front vowels;
2. for certain other speakers, before high and midfront vowels (Sapir, 1965: 5). The vowels of Diola-Fogny were given in Exercise 2(a) of Chapter 3. Compare the rules for the two sets of speakers.

5. In Cocama, we are told, 'each of the vowels may vary freely with its partially or completely voiceless counterpart word initially or in unstressed syllables' (Faust and Pike, 1959: 12). Examples are provided that show voiceless vowels: 1. initially before a voiceless stop, 2. finally after a voiceless stop, 3. between voiceless stops.

(a) Is the statement possibly too general? Are unstressed vowels between voiced consonants likely to be devoiced?
(b) Restate the quoted statement as a rule, assuming complete devoicing.
(c) Provide a rule that functions only in the three listed environments.

6. Cairo Arabic has a definite article /il-/, the /l/ of which is assimilated to a following /t d s z š ž n r/. The other consonants are /b f m l k g z x γ/, and the glides /h ʕ ʔ ħ w y/. (Based on Lehn and Abboud, 1965.) Examples:

kúrsi	*chair*	ilkúrsi	*the chair*
dars	*lesson*	iddárs	*the lesson*
innímra	*the grade*	ilmudárris	*the teacher*
issátr	*the line*	ilwá : gib	*the assignment*
ilbá : b	*the door*	ilqism	*the section*
iššánta	*the bag*	ilgé : b	*the pocket*

Consider the desirability of conceiving the assimilation rule as a change-producing device that does not affect /l/ before a noun such as /le : l/ *night*, and consequently should be formulated in such a way as to exclude the vacuous 'change' 1 > 1 in /il-le : l/.

CHAPTER 6

Rule Order

Phonological rules are ordered. For every utterance, the applicability of each rule is determined. If all or part of the string of phonological segments meets the structural description of the rule *n*, in accordance with the distinctiveness criterion, the rule is applied. If not, the rule is not applied. Then the applicability of rule *n* + 1 is determined, and so forth down the entire list of rules. A return is not made to any rule *n* from any rule *m* (where *m* > *n* + 1), even if at some later stage a form's structural description should come to fit that given in rule *n*. Rule cycles (discussed below) constitute an exception to this last statement, but even within rule cycles the order of the rules is fixed, and a return to rule *n* could not be made until the entire cycle is reapplied from beginning to end.

Finnish, for example, has the following rules:

(i)   e $\longrightarrow$ i   in environment   —‡

(ii)   t $\longrightarrow$ s   in environmenet   —i

(iii)   t $\longrightarrow$ d   in environment   —V(i)C$\begin{Bmatrix} C \\ \ddagger \end{Bmatrix}$

(iv)   ä $\longrightarrow$ null   in environment   —i (where [i] is 'plural').

Applied to the following underlying forms, the ordering of the rules determines the results. (Vowel harmony is ignored here.)

rule	käte *hand*	kätessä *in the* *hand*	kätissä *in the* *hands*	mätäissä *in rotten* (*ones*)	mätäinä *as rotten* (*ones*)	kätinä *as* *hands*
(i)	käti	—	—	—	—	—
(ii)	käsi	—	käsissä	—	—	käsinä
(iii)	—	kädessä	—	mädäissä	—	—
(iv)	—	—	—	mädissä	mätinä	—

Note that if (ii) were to precede (i), /käte/ would give *[käti]; if (iii) were to precede (ii), /kätissä/ would give *[kädissä] or *[käzissä], depending upon the feature formulation of the rule; if (iv) were to precede (ii) and (iii), /mätäissä/ would give *[mäsissä]. It should be clear that the derivation of the above results could be established without the use of ordered rules only through more complicated statements. Rule (iii) would have to ensure that the 'V' of the environment not be [i]; (ii) would have to list an additional environment that in effect duplicates rule (i), i.e., _e‡. More serious than the added complexity, however, is the loss of meaningful generalizations. Clearly, the change $t > s$ has nothing to do with [e]'s being in final position. The situation is even more complex than this simplified illustration indicates; cf. the phonetic forms [säde] *ray* (< /säteh/) and [ote] *grasp* (< /otteh/), which are in accord with the above ordered rules, but which would require a nonordered application of the above rules to include even more complicated environments.

A most extreme example of the achievement of generality and economy through the use of ordered rules is provided by Southern Paiute. The allophones of /š č/ are [s, š, c, č]. First, rules must be given that determine the compactness value of these two strident consonants in terms of the preceding and following vowels, where the underlying stridents and /o/ are taken as compact; thus,

$$(\text{v}) \begin{bmatrix} +\text{cns} \\ +\text{strid} \\ +\text{cnt} \end{bmatrix} \longrightarrow [-\text{cmp}] \Big/ \left\{ \begin{array}{l} \ddagger\!\!-\!\! \begin{bmatrix} -\text{cns} \\ +\text{voc} \\ \left\{\begin{array}{l}+\text{cmp}\\-\text{grve}\end{array}\right\} \end{bmatrix} \\[2ex] [-\text{grv}]\!\!-\!\! \begin{bmatrix} -\text{cns} \\ +\text{voc} \\ \alpha\text{grv} \\ \alpha\text{cmp} \end{bmatrix} \end{array} \right\}$$

(vi) $\begin{bmatrix} +\text{cns} \\ +\text{strid} \\ -\text{cnt} \end{bmatrix} \longrightarrow [-\text{cmp}] \;/\; \underline{} \begin{bmatrix} -\text{cns} \\ +\text{voc} \\ -\text{cmp} \\ -\text{grv} \end{bmatrix}$

i.e., š > s initially before [a, o, i] or after [i, a] before [i, o]; č > c
before [i]. If the results of these rules give two strident consonants in
contiguous syllables, they must agree in compactness in accordance
with the following rules:

(vii) $\begin{bmatrix} +\text{cns} \\ +\text{strid} \end{bmatrix} \longrightarrow [\alpha\text{cmp}] \;/\; \underline{}V \begin{bmatrix} +\text{cns} \\ +\text{strid} \\ -\text{cnt} \\ \alpha\text{cmp} \end{bmatrix}$

(viii) $\begin{bmatrix} +\text{cns} \\ +\text{strid} \end{bmatrix} \longrightarrow [\alpha\text{cmp}] \;/\; \begin{bmatrix} +\text{cns} \\ +\text{strid} \\ \alpha\text{cmp} \end{bmatrix}V\underline{}$

i.e., if the second of two strident consonants is an affricate (noncontinuant), it determines the compactness value for the pair; elsewhere
the first strident consonant determines compactness; thus /šiču-/ *nail* >
[siču-] by Rules (v–vi), and then [šiču-] by Rule (vii). Any attempt to
account for the occurrence of [š, s, č, c] without the use of the above
ordered rules would give statements of enormous complexity. Yet, in
traditional taxonomic phonemics, the price would have to be paid,
since the allophones of the two phonemes could not be described in
terms of these same allophones.

Even where taxonomic phonemics allows the use of ordered statements, the ordering conventions are rarely made explicit, and require
interpretation on the part of the reader, usually made possible by
listing examples of what the statements are supposed to reveal. In
"The Phonemes of Swahili", Zellig Harris gives the following allophonic description of the phonemes /p b n/ (Harris, 1951: 122–23;
certain environments have been numbered by RTH to facilitate
reference):

/p/	pᵉ	(1)	$\ddagger$—, —$\hat{V}$
	p	(2)	—$\hat{V}$
/b/	b		m—
	ɓ		
/n/	ŋ	(3)	—g, k
	nᵈ	(4)	—r
	ṇ	(5)	$\ddagger$—C
	n		

The only explicit statement of ordering is that 'if the last member in a phoneme group has no environment for it in the last column, then it occurs in all positions of C or V respectively ... except those in which other members of that phoneme occur' (122)—i.e., the 'elsewhere' situation, which covers [ɓ, n]. Inspection of Harris's fuller set of data listed on pp. 101–5 shows that two contradictory, unstated assumptions are made.

(a) Environment (1) must be considered to apply prior to and in exclusion of environment (2) (since the sequence $\pm$__$\dot{V}$ is possible).

(b) Environment (5) must be applied before (3) and (4), but in addition to them, since where both environments are met, the allophones of (3) and (4) are syllabic (i.e., [ŋᵈ, ŋ]).

By using ordered feature rules, the above Swahili data can be described in an explicit and general manner; thus (Rules (ix)–(xiv) below requiring knowledge of the abbreviatory conventions introduced in Chapter 7:

$$(\text{ix}) \quad \begin{bmatrix} +\text{obs} \\ -\text{cnt} \end{bmatrix} \longrightarrow [-\alpha\text{tns}] \; / \; \alpha \left\langle \begin{bmatrix} \underline{} \\ +\text{vce} \\ +\text{high} \end{bmatrix} \right\rangle$$

i.e., [g] is specified as nontense, and all other stops as tense.

$$(\text{x}) \quad \begin{bmatrix} +\text{obs} \\ -\text{cnt} \\ -\text{vce} \end{bmatrix} \longrightarrow [-\text{tns}] \; / \; [\quad\quad] - \begin{bmatrix} +\text{voc} \\ -\text{cns} \\ -\text{stress} \end{bmatrix}$$

i.e., voiceless stops are nontense noninitially (= after some segment) before an unstressed vowel.

$$(\text{xi}) \quad \begin{bmatrix} +\text{obs} \\ -\text{cnt} \\ +\text{vce} \\ \alpha\text{tns} \\ \beta\text{grv} \end{bmatrix} \longrightarrow [-\alpha\text{tns}] \; / \; \begin{bmatrix} +\text{nas} \\ \beta\text{grv} \end{bmatrix} -$$

i.e., voiced stops switch their tenseness after a nasal that agrees in graveness—thus, ɓ > b, g > g^ (strongly snapped) in the environment m__; ɗ > d in the environment n__. Harris' description misses this generalization when he gives the environment for [dʳ] as '__ù'—but his only examples show that it is always after [n] as well. Further, this illustrates how the type of economy measure used by Harris (cf. pp. 17–18), that is, the number of segment symbols, leads to the concealment of a generalization which can not be recovered on the basis of the descriptive statements of the analysis. Since in the environment 'n—' [d] is in free variation with [dʳ], the only significant environment for an obligatory [dʳ] would seem to be the one given by Harris; but once that decision is made, the generalization concerning the occurrence of tenseness with voiced stops can be found only by returning to the corpus of phonetic data.

$$\text{(xii)} \quad \begin{bmatrix} +\text{nas} \\ -\text{grv} \end{bmatrix} \longrightarrow \begin{bmatrix} \alpha\text{grv} \\ \beta\text{high} \end{bmatrix} / \underline{\qquad} \begin{bmatrix} +\text{obs} \\ -\text{cnt} \\ \alpha\text{grv} \\ \beta\text{ high} \end{bmatrix}$$

i.e., [n] (but not [m]) assimilates to a following obstruent in place of articulation.

$$\text{(xiii)} \quad [+\text{nas}] \longrightarrow [+\text{syl}] / \#\_C$$

i.e., nasals are syllabic initially before a consonant—thus [n̩ᵈ] and [ŋ̍], not covered explicitly by Harris.

$$\text{(xiv)} \quad \text{SD:} \quad \begin{bmatrix} +\text{nas} \\ \alpha\text{grv} \end{bmatrix} \begin{bmatrix} +\text{cns} \\ -\text{obs} \\ -\text{nas} \\ \beta\text{cnt} \end{bmatrix}$$
$$\qquad\qquad\qquad 1 \qquad\qquad\; 2$$

Condition: If α is '−', β is '+'.

$$\text{SC: } 1 \longrightarrow 1 \; {}^{\wedge} \begin{bmatrix} 1 \\ -\text{nas} \end{bmatrix}$$

i.e., if a nasal is followed by a liquid (except for [nl], where α is '−' and β is '−'), a voiced stop homorganic with the nasal is inserted between them (i.e., with all the features of the nasal except nasality; the sign '^' indicates concatenation and is not a symbol in the string).

Historical linguistics and dialect geography provide further support for the claim that languages employ ordered phonological rules. Paul Postal (1965) has demonstrated cases of sound change in Oneida and Mohawk that resulted either from a change in the order of rules already present in the language or from the insertion of a rule at a point that does not correspond to the known chronology of changes in the language. Paul Kiparsky (1967a) shows the necessity for recognizing similar nonchronological rule insertions for explaining Greek stress phenomena and 'Lachmann's law' in Latin. Without the recognition of ordered rules as phonological units, the changes involved cannot be explained in any reasonable manner, in accord with a general theory of language structure.

In recent years many examples of dialect differences based upon the relative ordering of the same rules have been found, e.g., Keyser, 1963; Saporta, 1965; King, 1966. For three Dacorumanian dialects described by E. Vasiliu (1966)—say, A, B, C—within a taxonomic (biunique) phonemic approach, dialects A and C are found to have the same phoneme inventory; thus both have, among others, the voiceless noncontinuant obstruents /t č k'/. By contrast, dialect B lacks the phoneme /k'/. In all three dialects, /t/ does not contrast with the other two obstruents in question before /i e/. In generative terms, however, all three dialects have the same inventory of underlying systematic phonemes, represented at some stage by [t č k']. The various dialects have grammars containing the following rules in various orders:

(a) dentals are palatalized before a front vowel (t > t', also n > ń)
(b) k' > č
(c) t' > k'
(d) t' > č
(e) $\begin{Bmatrix} t' \\ k' \end{Bmatrix} > č$

All dialects share Rule (a). Dialect C has Rule (d), whereas A has the ordered pair of Rules (b)-(c). Thus, in C, underlying /t/ before a front vowel is realized as [č]; in A, on the other hand, [k'] is realized as [č], and /t/ before a front vowel as [k']. Dialect B is best treated synchronically by Rule (e), which, in distinctive feature terms, is more general than either (b) or (d). The results of these rules are illustrated in the following table:

	t'	č	k'
dialect A	k'	č	č
dialect B	č	č	č
dialect C	č	č	k'

Although the taxonomic similarity of A and C is fortuitous, B is clearly related to either A or C or both. In attempting to find more meaningful dialect relationships, we note that B can be described alternatively as:

1. Sharing Rules (b) and (c) with A, but in the order (c)-(b); 2. Sharing
Rule (b) with A and Rule (d) with C; 3. As having borrowed and
generalized either Rule (b) or Rule (d) by the deletion of features from
their structural description (in the manner described in Harms, 1967).

EXERCISES

1. Re-examine the taxonomic description of Assiniboine given as Exercise 1
   to Chapter 2 with regard to the problem of rule order.

   (a) Do problems of order arise in conjunction with the specification of
   allophones (cf. especially the environments of /t/ and /p/)?

   (b) How would environment (3) probably be treated within a generative
   framework?

   (c) In light of the use of 'elsewhere' in this description, which follows
   standard taxonomic practice, evaluate the claim that 'one major
   difference between taxonomic phonemics and generative phonology is
   that the latter allows ordered statements of description'.

2. The following changes in the development of Slavic are generally assumed
   to have occurred in the order:

   I. Velar obstruents (i.e., /k g x/) became strident palatals before front
   vowels or [y], and [y] was lost after such palatals.

   II. [oy] diphthongs became [æ] or [i]. The conditions are obscure. There
   was a previous [i], but no [æ].

   III. Velar obstruents became strident apicals before [æ] and new [i].

   Note the Old Slavic paradigms:

	friend	*terror*	*darkness*
nominative	drugŭ	straxŭ	mrakŭ
genitive	druga	straxa	mraka
locative	druʒæ	strasæ	mracæ
vocative	druže	straše	mrače
nom. pl.	druʒi	strasi	mraci

Also: [družina] *comrades*, [strašiti] *to frighten*, [strašĭnŭ] *terrible*, [mračĭnŭ]
dark. ([ŭ ĭ] are lax as opposed to tense [u i].) Will the purely synchronic
description of Old Slavic benefit by incorporating the above historical
changes as rules? Will the synchronic rule order be the same as the historical sequence of changes? Give the underlying form for [cælŭ] *whole*.

3. Menomini (based on Bloomfield, 1939)

(a) ōs *canoe*
(b) ōnan *canoes*
(c) otōs *his canoe*   Take as given:
(d) ketōs *your* (sing.) *canoe*   /ōne/ *canoe*
(e) ketōnowaw *your* (pl.) *canoe*   /-owaw/ *non-first person*
(f) otōnowawan *their canoes*   *plural possessor*
(g) onɛ̄h *his hand*   /o-/ *third person possessor*
(h) nenɛ̄h *my hand*
(i) kenɛ̄hkowawan *your* (pl.) *hands*
(j) kenɛ̄hkenawan *our* (inclusive) *hands*

Note: Menomini requires, among others, the two rules:

1. ɛ > e in initial syllables (except before a [ʔC] or [hC] sequence).
2. n > s before e.

Establish the underlying forms of the above words so that each morpheme has only one underlying representation, the necessary rules (including the two above), and the order in which they apply.

4. Estonian:

	knob	doll	corner	black	death	flower
nom.	nuk : :	nuk : :	nuk : :	mus : t	sur : m	lil : :
gen.	nukki	nukku	nukka	musta	surma	lille

	smell	thigh	wrong	shank	apple	ear
nom.	hai : s	rei : s	vä : : r	sä : : r	əu : n	kər : v
gen.	haisu	reise	vä : ra	sä : re	əuna	kərva

	nest	father	meat	beauty	junk	reef
nom.	pesa	isa	liha	ilu	kol'i	kaŕi
gen.	pesa	isa	liha	ilu	kol'i	kaŕi

	herd	matter	oven	fruit	pillow	
nom.	kaŕi	aśi	ahi	vil'i	pat'i	
gen.	kaŕya	aśya	ahyu	vil'ya	pat'ya	

	top	wart	rain	spot	juice	gristle
nom.	lat : f	käs : N	vih : M	täh : N	mah : ł	kəh : R
gen.	latva	käsna	vihma	tähni	mahla	kəhri

[N M R] are voiceless.
[:] indicates one additional mora of length belonging to the preceding segment.

[C:] across syllable boundaries have been transcribed as geminate [CC] clusters.

Monosyllabic words (except ‡CV‡) contain an extra mora of length.

The genitive may be considered to end in a consonant /h/ which is lost in final position.

(a) Posit underlying systematic phonemic transcriptions and a set of ordered rules that together account for the above data. (Consider specifically the treatment of long segments as geminate clusters, and the need for both /i/ and /y/ phonemes.)

(b) Evaluate the analysis which led to the following statement (Harms, 1962: 33):

> 'The recognition of /f š/ as phonemes is necessitated by their occurrence in a handful of recent foreign loans; and consequently, they do not have a wide or symmetrical distribution. Once established, however, /f/ also comes to occur in native Estonian words in morphophonemic alternation with /v/ in those positions for which voiced consonants have voiceless allophones.'

Consequently, in a taxonomic study such as Harms, 1962, the alternation of /f/ and /v/ is seen as morphophonemic, for which a special symbol /W/ is set up, and a special rule is given in the section "Segmental Morphophonemes" (p. 49); whereas the voiceless liquids and nasals are seen as allophones and are listed in the section "Consonants" (pp. 24–25).

CHAPTER 7

Abbreviatory Devices

Numerous conventions for reducing several rules to a single rule or for deleting irrelevant information from rules have been devised. We must bear in mind here the role of the simplicity metric in insuring that the phonology will reflect the most highly valued generalizations of the language. The goal is not to collapse rules in order to save ink. Any device that leads to a more economical description must be shown to lead, at the same time, to desirable generalizations in terms of how that device is to be counted. Outside of the simplicity metric, economy in the description has no real meaning.

The following notational conventions are in common usage and have been claimed to reflect valid linguistic generalizations.

1. Parentheses indicate optional elements that are whole segments (but not features within segments); e.g.,

$$(i) \quad \begin{bmatrix} +voc \\ -cns \end{bmatrix} \longrightarrow [-grv] \; / \; \_\_ \; ([+cns]) \begin{bmatrix} +voc \\ -cns \\ -grv \\ +high \end{bmatrix}$$

which is an abbreviation of the sequence of two rules:

$$(ii) \quad \begin{bmatrix} +voc \\ -cns \end{bmatrix} \longrightarrow [-grv] \; / \; \_\_ \; [+cns] \begin{bmatrix} +voc \\ -cns \\ -grv \\ +high \end{bmatrix}$$

57

$$\text{(iii)} \quad \begin{bmatrix} +\text{voc} \\ -\text{cns} \end{bmatrix} \longrightarrow [-\text{grv}] \ / \ \_\_ \begin{bmatrix} +\text{voc} \\ -\text{cns} \\ -\text{grv} \\ +\text{high} \end{bmatrix}$$

i.e., vowels are front either immediately before [i] or separated from it by a single consonant.

With all abbreviatory devices of this type it is necessary to make explicit the order in which the device is to be expanded. In the case of parentheses, the rule is to be interpreted as an ordered series of rules, longer expansions preceding shorter ones; thus: (i) is to be applied as Rule (ii) followed by Rule (iii). (See also the paragraph on disjunctive ordering below.)

2. Braces abbreviate sequences of partially similar rules.

$$\text{(iv)} \quad \begin{bmatrix} +\text{obs} \\ -\text{grv} \\ -\text{high} \end{bmatrix} \longrightarrow [+\text{cnt}] \ / \ \left\{ \begin{matrix} \_\_\_ \begin{bmatrix} +\text{voc} \\ -\text{cns} \\ +\text{high} \\ -\text{flt} \end{bmatrix} \\ \ddagger\_\_\_[+\text{cns}] \end{matrix} \right\}$$

i.e., of the apical obstruents [t, s], only [s] occurs before [i] or initially before a consonant. Rule (iv) will change any [t] to [s] in these environments and also will apply vacuously to [s], which does not change. If we were to write the rule only to operate upon [t], the rule would require an additional feature '−cnt' on the left of the arrow—which in this instance serves no purpose.

$$\text{(v)} \quad \left[\left\{ \begin{matrix} +\text{cns} \\ -\text{voc} \end{matrix} \right\} \right] \longrightarrow [-\text{stress}]$$

i.e., any segment that is either consonantal or nonvocalic is unstressed.

The further subgrouping of features within a segment with the use of braces, as in (v), can be indicated with brackets (still referring to the same segment), parentheses, or angled parentheses; e.g., (b) and (c) express equivalent abbreviations of (a):

$$\text{(a)} \left\{ \begin{matrix} \begin{bmatrix} +\text{syl} \\ +\text{nas} \end{bmatrix} \\ \begin{bmatrix} +\text{syl} \\ +\text{grv} \\ -\text{flt} \end{bmatrix} \end{matrix} \right\} \qquad \text{(b)} \left[\left\{ \begin{matrix} ([+\text{nas}]) \\ \begin{bmatrix} +\text{grv} \\ -\text{flt} \end{bmatrix} \end{matrix} \right\} \right] \qquad \text{(c)} \left[\begin{matrix} +\text{syl} \\ \left(\begin{matrix} +\text{nas} \\ \left\langle \begin{matrix} +\text{grv} \\ -\text{flt} \end{matrix} \right\rangle \end{matrix} \right) \end{matrix} \right]$$

The use of angled parentheses is not recommended, however, since care must be taken to avoid confusion with the angled-parenthesis convention discussed below.

With braces, the convention for expansion calls for the interpretation of the rule as a series of ordered rules with higher-line expansions preceding lower-line expansions. In (iv) and (v) the order of expansion would not make any difference, but note the following rule:

(vi) $\qquad [-\text{obs}] \longrightarrow \begin{Bmatrix} [-\text{nas}] \\ [+\text{nas}] \ / \ \begin{bmatrix} \underline{\quad\quad} \\ +\text{cns} \\ -\text{voc} \end{bmatrix} \end{Bmatrix}$

i.e., nonobstruent consonants are nonnasal except for those which are consonantal and nonvocalic. Here the correct results are obtained only if the above convention for expansion is followed. First, all nonobstruents are specified as nonnasal; then, by the second line of the braces, the special case reverses its nasality to 'plus'. (In the second expansion $[-\text{obs}]$, $[+\text{nas}]$, and $[\underline{\quad}, +\text{cns}, -\text{voc}]$ all refer to the same segment.)

Since square brackets are reserved for the designation of segments, the square brackets of earlier generative studies (cf. Bach, 1964: 18) have been replaced by numbered braces—i.e., where the nth line in one pair of numbered braces is chosen, the nth line in all other braces of the same number must be chosen. The following rule for inserting German second-person verb suffixes (simplified from Ross, 1966) illustrates the use of numbered braces:

(vii) $\quad \emptyset \longrightarrow \text{ĕ} \begin{Bmatrix} \text{s} \\ \emptyset \end{Bmatrix} \quad \text{t} \ / \ ) \atop \underset{1 \quad 1}{} \quad \underset{1}{\text{Stem}} + \underset{\underset{1}{}}{\begin{bmatrix} \overline{+2\text{nd}} \\ \begin{Bmatrix} +\text{singular} \\ -\text{singular} \end{Bmatrix} \end{bmatrix}} \underset{1}{}$

The structural description refers to syntactic bracketing (i.e., the rightmost boundary of a stem) and the morpheme features '2nd' and 'singular' to provide phonetic substance for the morpheme segment indicated by the brackets containing these morpheme features. A morpheme segment that is '+2nd, +singular' is realized as [ĕst]; one that is '+2nd, −singular', as [ĕt].

8. Greek-letter ('alpha') variables (cf. Halle, 1962a). A variable is a device that can stand for given elements of the string of phonological symbols in the structural description. Greek-letter variables stand for

the plus and minus values of features. They indicate agreement or dis-
agreement of values in various parts of the rule; e.g.,

$$\text{(viii)} \quad [+\text{nas}] \longrightarrow \begin{bmatrix} \alpha\text{high} \\ \beta\text{grv} \end{bmatrix} / - \begin{bmatrix} +\text{obs} \\ +\text{cnt} \\ \alpha\text{high} \\ \beta\text{grv} \end{bmatrix}$$

i.e., a nasal must have the same buccal and graveness values as a following stop. It abbreviates the four rules:

$$\text{(a)} \quad [+\text{nas}] \longrightarrow \begin{bmatrix} -\text{high} \\ +\text{grv} \end{bmatrix} / - \begin{bmatrix} -\text{cnt} \\ +\text{obs} \\ -\text{high} \\ +\text{grv} \end{bmatrix} \quad (\text{N} > \text{m} \, / \, \text{—p, b})$$

$$\text{(b)} \quad [+\text{nas}] \longrightarrow \begin{bmatrix} -\text{high} \\ -\text{grv} \end{bmatrix} / - \begin{bmatrix} +\text{obs} \\ -\text{cnt} \\ -\text{high} \\ -\text{grv} \end{bmatrix} \quad (\text{N} > \text{n} \, / \, \text{—t, d})$$

$$\text{(c)} \quad [+\text{nas}] \longrightarrow \begin{bmatrix} +\text{high} \\ -\text{grv} \end{bmatrix} / - \begin{bmatrix} +\text{obs} \\ -\text{cnt} \\ +\text{high} \\ -\text{grv} \end{bmatrix} \quad (\text{N} > \text{ń} \, / \, \text{—č, ž})$$

$$\text{(d)} \quad [+\text{nas}] \longrightarrow \begin{bmatrix} +\text{high} \\ +\text{grv} \end{bmatrix} / - \begin{bmatrix} +\text{obs} \\ -\text{cnt} \\ +\text{high} \\ +\text{grv} \end{bmatrix} \quad (\text{N} > \text{ŋ} \, / \, \text{—k, g})$$

Thus the generalization of the homorganic assimilation of nasals, discussed in Chapter 2, is captured in (viii) through the use of alpha-type
variables.

$$\text{(ix)} \qquad \begin{bmatrix} \alpha\text{cns} \\ \alpha\text{voc} \end{bmatrix} \longrightarrow [+\text{syl}] \, / \, \text{C\_C}$$

i.e., glides and resonants (as in Indo-European) are syllabic between
consonants. Here the structural description requires that the consonantal

and vocalic values be either both 'plus' (liquids and nasals) or both
'minus' (y and w).

$$
\text{(x)} \qquad \begin{bmatrix} +\text{voc} \\ -\text{cns} \\ \alpha\text{grv} \end{bmatrix} \longrightarrow [\alpha\text{flat}]
$$

i.e., front vowels are unrounded ([−grv, −flt]; back vowels are
rounded ([+grv, +flt]).

Where more than one relationship is needed, other Greek letters
may be used; e.g.,

$$
\text{(xi)} \qquad \begin{bmatrix} +\text{voc} \\ -\text{cns} \\ \alpha\text{grv} \\ \alpha\text{flt} \\ \beta\text{high} \end{bmatrix} \longrightarrow [\beta\text{tns}]
$$

i.e., in vowels that are front unrounded or back rounded, the tenseness
value is made to agree with the highness value ([i, u] are tense; [e, o],
nontense). There is no connection between the 'α' values and the 'β'
values in this rule, or in (viii) above.

Greek-letter variables can be negated to indicate a lack of agreement; e.g., '−α' indicates a value of 'minus' where 'α' stands for 'plus';
it indicates a value of 'plus' where 'α' stands for 'minus'. Thus:

$$
\text{(xii)} \qquad\qquad [\alpha\text{vce}] \longrightarrow [-\alpha\text{tns}]
$$

i.e., voiced segments are nontense; voiceless segments, tense.
Or for dissimilation:

$$
\text{(xiii)} \qquad [+\text{obs}] \longrightarrow [-\alpha\text{cnt}] \ / \ -\begin{bmatrix} +\text{obs} \\ \alpha\text{cnt} \end{bmatrix}
$$

i.e., in a sequence of two contiguous obstruents, the first must have an
opposite value for continuance from the second.

An 'alpha-switching' rule is one in which a Greek-letter value for a
given feature on the left of the arrow is reversed in the brackets on the
right of the arrow. These generally lead to 'flip-flops' or shifts; thus,
Middle English is likely to have had a rule such as the following
(posited for J. Hart; Halle, 1966):

$$
\text{(xiv)} \qquad \begin{bmatrix} \alpha\text{high} \\ -\text{low} \end{bmatrix} \longrightarrow [-\alpha\text{high}] \ / \ \begin{bmatrix} +\text{tns} \\ +\text{stress} \end{bmatrix}
$$

i.e., i > e, u > o, e > i, o > u. Southern Paiute velar continuants show
the shift [ɣ] > [x], [x] > [x:]:

(xv) $\begin{bmatrix} +\text{obs} \\ +\text{high} \\ +\text{grv} \\ +\text{cnt} \\ \alpha\text{vce} \end{bmatrix} \longrightarrow \begin{bmatrix} -\alpha\text{long} \\ -\text{vce} \end{bmatrix}$

From the above examples it should be apparent that alpha-switching
rules cannot be allowed to reapply to their own output. In the case of
(xiv) this would lead to an unending series of i > e > i . . . , etc. With
(xv), (ɣ) would become [x], which in turn would become, incorrectly,
[x:]. To prevent this, a general convention—the noniterative rule convention—has been adopted, which specifies that the output of one application of any given rule cannot be required for subsequent applications
of the same rule, nor a rule reapply to its own output.

A word of caution may be in order for those unfamiliar with the use
of alpha-type variables. They are never used to indicate that a given
feature is not simply relevant to a rule—in the sense that it makes no
difference whether alpha is 'plus' or 'minus'. There will be, then, no rules
containing only a single alpha or a single beta. Beta is never used in the
sense of 'the opposite value of alpha' (properly expressed only as '−α').
4. Other general variables, usually X, Y, Z; sometimes also '. . .',
stand for arbitrary sequences—possibly null—in the environments of
rules, thus; Finnish vowel harmony can be stated as:

(xvi) $\begin{bmatrix} +\text{voc} \\ -\text{cns} \\ -\text{act} \end{bmatrix} \longrightarrow [\alpha\text{grv}] \ / \ \begin{bmatrix} +\text{voc} \\ -\text{cns} \\ -\text{act} \\ \alpha\text{grv} \end{bmatrix} \text{X}\_\_\_$

i.e., any Finnish nonacute vowel agrees in graveness with the first nonacute vowel in the same word, assuming that this rule is limited to occurrence within word boundaries (cf. the section on boundary constraints
below). This rule is an abbreviation for as many rules as there are forms
of X (i.e., segment sequences that can separate two nonacute vowels
and null). The convention for expanding X-type variables is that of representing an ordered series of rules such that any longer stretch of
segments that X can contain will be applied before any shorter sequence;
e.g., given a situation in which X stands for the string 'a b c', X will

first take the value 'a b c', then 'a b', then 'a', and finally 'null'. For the Finnish word [tuOnelA]—where [u O A] are nonacute and [O A] are unspecified for graveness—with the first application of Rule (xvi), X = [Onel] and [A] > [a] (+grave); with the second application, X is null and [O] > [o].

5. 'C' and 'V'. For the universal classes 'consonant' and 'vowel', the symbols 'C' and 'V' are used instead of the necessary feature specifications (cf. Chapter 4 above). A vowel is any segment that is nonconsonantal and also vocalic or syllabic; all other segments are consonants. Thus Rule (i) above could also be given as:

$$(xvii) \qquad V \longrightarrow [-grv] \ / \ \underline{\hspace{1em}} \ (C) \begin{bmatrix} +voc \\ -cns \\ -grv \\ +high \end{bmatrix}$$

How to count these symbols within the simplicity metric is not clear— i.e., whether they are to be considered as mere symbolic abbreviations, and to be counted the same as the features that they replace, or as generalizations to be reflected in the metric.

6. Upper- and lower-limit specifications are frequently used to deal with optional repeated sequences of a given form. The lower limit is indicated by subscript numerals immediately following the symbol. The absence of a lower limit is expressed by a subscript zero. An upper limit is indicated by a raised numeral; the absence of an upper limit is indicated by the absence of a raised numeral in the presence of a specified lower limit; e.g.,

$$C_0 = \text{any number of C's or none}$$
$$C_1 = \text{at least one C}$$
$$(C_0V)_0 = \text{any number of } C_0V \text{ sequences or none.}$$

$C_1^1 =$ one and only one C, however, is not the same as the symbol 'C', since C_1^1 excludes the possibility of a preceding (or following) consonant (unless explicitly indicated); e.g., '__C' is to be read 'before any consonant (regardless of what follows)', but '__C_1^1' in effect limits the environment to 'before a single consonant (and not before a consonant cluster)'. $C_0^1 =$ at most one C, differs from '(C)' in the same manner as C_1^1 from C.

The following rule unstresses all odd-numbered vowels counting from word initial position (as in Southern Paiute):

$$\text{(xviii)}\qquad V \longrightarrow [-\text{stress}] \;/\; \ddagger \; (C_0 V C_0 V)_0 C_0 \text{---}$$

As above, the convention for expanding upper-lower limit abbreviations requires that the longest instance be applied first.

7. Disjunctive ordering and the noniterative rule convention. With parentheses having a specified upper limit, including plain parentheses (X), a convention of disjunctive ordering is applied. According to this convention, only the earliest subrule expansion applicable to a given form may apply to that form, even if later subrule expansions would otherwise (in terms of their structural description) appear applicable; e.g., for a rule $a \longrightarrow c \;/\; a(a)$__, the forms *aacb* and *aaab* would become *accb* and *aacb* respectively, but the rule cannot reapply to its *aacb* ($< aaab$) output, even though the structural description would appear to be identical to the *aacb* to which the rule had not previously applied. Note the Latin stress rule:

$$\text{(xix)}\qquad V \longrightarrow [+\text{stress}] \;/\; \text{---}C_0((\begin{bmatrix} +\text{voc} \\ -\text{cns} \\ -\text{lng} \end{bmatrix}.)C_0 V C_0)\ddagger$$

i.e.; (a) the antepenultimate vowel is stressed if the penultimate vowel is short in an open syllable (where '.' indicates syllable boundary); (b) otherwise the penultimate vowel is stressed; (c) the single vowel of a monosyllable is stressed. Without this convention, (b) and (c) expansions of (xix) would introduce unwanted stresses on words with antepenultimate stress. Note, however, that the convention does not apply to the Southern Paiute stress Rule (xviii), since its parentheses have no upper limit.

Braces, on the other hand, provide for conjunctive ordering of abbreviated rules, since a lower line within a given pair of braces may contain a structural description that is also included within some earlier structural description; e.g., in Rule (vi) above, a nonobstruent, consonantal, nonvocalic segment is a subset of the class of nonobstruents.

The expansion conventions, disjunctive and conjunctive abbreviations are closely related to the noniterative rule convention (NIR)—i.e., the constraint that prevents rules from reapplying to their own output, specifying that the output of one application of a given rule can not be required for subsequent applications of the same rule. The expansion of parentheses, X-type variables, and upper/lower limit terms will always provide subrules that are in accord with the NIR convention; e.g., Rule (xviii) applied to a sequence of stressed vowels would operate as follows:

(a)	Given	ǂ	v́ v́ v́ v́ v́
(b)	1st application	ǂ	v́ v́ v́ v́ v̆
(c)	2nd application	ǂ	v́ v́ v̆ v́ v̆
(d)	3rd application	ǂ	v̆ v́ v̆ v́ v̆

Note that the second and third applications of the rule are independent of any prior application.

With braces, however, the noniterative rule convention is applied to the separate subrule expansions rather than to the rule as a whole. Compare (xviii) with the following rule expressing the same constraint on stress occurrence, but which violates the NIR convention:

$$(xx) \quad V \longrightarrow [-\text{stress}] \; / \; \left\{ \begin{bmatrix} +\text{voc} \\ -\text{cns} \\ -\text{stress} \end{bmatrix}^{\overset{\text{ǂ}}{}} C_0 V \right\} C_0 \underline{\hspace{2cm}}$$

Applied to the above sequence (a), (xx) shows:

(b′)	1st application	v̆ v́ v́ v́ v́
(c′)	2nd application	v̆ v́ v̆ v́ v́
(d′)	3rd application	v̆ v́ v̆ v́ v̆

The output of the first application, based on line one of the environment, is required as the environment determining the second application (line two), the second for the third, etc. For (xviii), each application of the rules corresponds to a different subrule; for (xx), all applications except the first correspond to the same subrule. The violation, then, occurs not at the point at which line one of (xx) is required for line two, but where one output of line two is required for a subsequent application of itself.

Although (xviii) and (xx) do not differ significantly in economy, a rule like (xx) would require an ad-hoc condition permitting the violation of the NIR convention in this instance, or one that applies the convention only to alpha-switching rules (see above).

Compare also rule (vi) above, which does not violate the NIR convention as interpreted here with conjunctive ordering, since each of the rules derived by expanding the abbreviation satisfies the conditions of the NIR convention.

8. The 'angled parentheses' $\langle \ldots \rangle$ indicate elements in one part of the rule that require the presence of elements within angles in another part of the rule. Capanahua, for example, requires a rule such as (xxi), which states that if two strident consonants are separated only by a vowel, the second strident must agree with the first in compactness ('αcmp')—e.g., [caca] *fish*, [cispop] *ashes*; and, *moreover*, if they have the same continuance value ('βcnt'), then they also agree in flatness ('γflt')—e.g., [šašo] *tray*; but [čašo] *deer*, where [š] : [š] contrast in flatness (Loos, 1967).

$$
\text{(xxi)} \quad
\begin{bmatrix} +\text{strid} \\ \langle \beta\text{cnt} \rangle \end{bmatrix}
\longrightarrow
\begin{bmatrix} \alpha\text{cmp} \\ \langle \gamma\text{flt} \rangle \end{bmatrix}
\Big/
\begin{bmatrix} +\text{strid} \\ \alpha\text{cmp} \\ \langle \beta\text{cnt} \\ \gamma\text{flt} \rangle \end{bmatrix}
[+\text{syl}]\_\_
$$

The expansion convention here requires that the subrules be disjunctively ordered, the fullest expansion coming first. Thus Rule (xxi) expresses two subrules. The first subrule includes all the features in angled parentheses; the second, only those features not in angles.

More than two rules can be abbreviated by the use of subscript numerals (not to be confused with lower-limit numerals). Thus the following Alsatian German rule (Becker, 1967) indicates that before [y] all vowels become nonhigh, and, in addition, if a vowel is rounded, it must be a front vowel; if it is originally high, it must be tensed.

$$
\text{(xxii)} \quad
\begin{bmatrix} +\text{syl} \\ \langle +\text{flt} \rangle_1 \\ \langle +\text{dif} \rangle_2 \end{bmatrix}
\longrightarrow
\begin{bmatrix} -\text{dif} \\ \langle -\text{grv} \rangle_1 \\ \langle +\text{tns} \rangle_2 \end{bmatrix}
\Big/ \_\_
\begin{bmatrix} -\text{cns} \\ -\text{syl} \\ -\text{grv} \end{bmatrix}
$$

The expansion of (xxii) gives four subrules, where the SD contains: (a) both '+flt' and '+dif'; (b) only '+flt'; (c) only '+dif'; (d) neither '+flt' nor '+dif'.

Unless special conditions are imposed, any $\langle \ldots \rangle_i$ of the structural change requires the presence of all other $\langle \ldots \rangle_i$ in the structural description.

9. The deletion of the environment bar '_' has been suggested as a meaningful abbreviation in situations where an 'either after or before' relationship exists (Bach, 1966). Thus, '/ $\begin{Bmatrix} \text{a}\_\_ \\ \_\_\text{a} \end{Bmatrix}$' can be reduced to

'/ a'. For example, Dutch has the rule:

$$(\text{xxiii}) \qquad [+\text{obs}] \longrightarrow [+\text{vce}] \ / \ \begin{bmatrix} +\text{obs} \\ -\text{cnt} \\ +\text{vce} \end{bmatrix}$$

i.e., obstruents are voiced after or before a voiced stop.

In environments that contain more than one element, e.g., '$a_1 a_2 \ldots a_n$', the expansion results in two ordered rules, the second environment being the mirror-image of the first; thus, '$a_1 a_2 \ldots a_n$' is expanded as :1. '$a_1 a_2 \ldots a_n$__' and 2. '__$a_n \ldots a_2 a_1$'. For example, Modern Greek has the following vowel cluster reduction rule:

$$(\text{xxiv}) \qquad V \longrightarrow \text{null} \ / \ \begin{pmatrix} a \\ o \\ u \\ i \end{pmatrix} +$$

i.e., first, any vowel next to [a] across morpheme boundary is deleted; then any vowel next to [o]; then vowels next to [u]; finally, vowels next to [i]. Note that the expansion of the braces must be made before the expansion to the environment bar; thus:

$$\text{first:} \ \begin{pmatrix} a+ \\ o+ \\ u+ \\ i+ \end{pmatrix}, \quad \text{and then:} \ \begin{pmatrix} a+\_ \\ \_+a \\ o+\_ \\ \_+o \\ \text{etc.} \end{pmatrix}$$

10. Environments may be compounded; e.g.,

$$/\_a/ \ \begin{Bmatrix} c\_ \\ \_d \end{Bmatrix}$$

may be considered an abbreviation of the two environments: 1. c__a, 2. __da; i.e., the second environment, with its environment bar, is inserted within the first environment at the place indicated by its environment bar; e.g.

$$> / \ \begin{Bmatrix} c\_ \\ \_d \end{Bmatrix} a \qquad\qquad > / \ \begin{Bmatrix} c\_a \\ \_da \end{Bmatrix}$$

A low-level phonetic rule in Estonian specifies that obstruents are shortened (assigned a value of '−2 long'; cf. the use of numerical values in Chapter 9) in the environment of another obstruent when in a three-consonant cluster; thus,

(xxv)   [+obs] ⟶ [−2 long] / C/ [+obs]

Employing the environment bar expansion, this results in the four environments:

1. C[+obs]__,   2. C__[+obs],   3. [+obs]__C,   4. __[+obs]C

11. Under certain circumstances a shift of format to that generally employed in stating transformational rules is recommended; e.g., instead of ab ⟶ cd / __e, the following format is used:

$$\begin{array}{lll} \text{SD} & \text{(structural description):} & \text{a b e} \\ & & \text{1 2 3} \\ \text{SC} & \text{(structural change):} & 1 \longrightarrow c \\ & & 2 \longrightarrow d \end{array}$$

This is especially desirable where more than one segment is altered by a rule. For example, in one possible analysis for Southern Paiute, a sequence of an unstressed vowel plus [h] drops the [h] and devoices the vowel; e.g., V̆h > V̥̆. The attempt to handle this with a rule such as (xxvi) does not meaningfully express the underlying generalization, since all the vowel features must be presented on the left and also be rewritten on the right.

$$(xxvi) \quad \begin{bmatrix} -\text{cns} \\ +\text{voc} \\ -\text{stress} \\ \alpha\text{cmp} \\ \beta\text{grv} \\ \gamma\text{flt} \end{bmatrix} \begin{bmatrix} -\text{cns} \\ -\text{voc} \\ +\text{cnt} \end{bmatrix} \longrightarrow \begin{bmatrix} -\text{cns} \\ +\text{voc} \\ -\text{stress} \\ -\text{voice} \\ \alpha\text{cmp} \\ \beta\text{grv} \\ \gamma\text{flt} \end{bmatrix}$$

A rule such as (xxvii) could not clearly indicate this change—perhaps it is the vowel that is lost, with [h] becoming voiceless.

$$(xxvii) \quad \begin{bmatrix} -\text{cns} \\ +\text{voc} \\ -\text{stress} \end{bmatrix} \begin{bmatrix} -\text{cns} \\ -\text{voc} \\ +\text{cnt} \end{bmatrix} \longrightarrow [-\text{vce}]$$

Nor would the addition of [−cns, +voc] to the right of the arrow make it clear that a new voiceless vowel, incorporating the flatness, graveness, and compactness values of [h], had not been created.

Still another approach, one that I had adopted in an earlier analysis of Southern Paiute, is to treat the change in two steps: 1. V $\longrightarrow$ [−vce] / __h; and 2. h $\longrightarrow$ null /__[V, −vce]. The structural description is essentially the same in both rules; and, since there is no other source of voiceless vowel plus [h], the fact of the interdependence of these two rules is obscured.

Rule (xxviii), on the other hand, expresses the above change without ambiguity and irrelevant features:

(xxviii)
$$\text{SD:} \quad \begin{bmatrix} -\text{cns} \\ +\text{voc} \\ -\text{stress} \end{bmatrix} \quad \begin{bmatrix} -\text{cns} \\ -\text{voc} \\ +\text{cnt} \end{bmatrix}$$
$$1 \qquad\qquad 2$$

$$\text{SC:} \quad \begin{array}{l} 1 \longrightarrow [-\text{vce}] \\ 2 \longrightarrow \text{null} \end{array}$$

A somewhat modified version of (xxviii), such as (xxviii′), might also be used in rules of this type.

(xxviii′)
$$\begin{bmatrix} -\text{cns} \\ +\text{voc} \\ -\text{stress} \end{bmatrix} \quad \begin{bmatrix} -\text{cns} \\ -\text{voc} \\ +\text{cnt} \end{bmatrix} \longrightarrow [-\text{vce}] \; \text{null}$$

The following Southern Paiute rule also is best handled with this format:

(xxix)
$$\text{SD:} \quad \begin{bmatrix} -\text{cns} \\ +\text{voc} \end{bmatrix} \quad \begin{bmatrix} -\text{cns} \\ +\text{voc} \\ +\text{stress} \end{bmatrix}$$
$$1 \qquad\qquad 2$$

$$\text{SC:} \quad \begin{array}{l} 1 \longrightarrow [+\text{stress}] \\ 2 \longrightarrow [-\text{stress}] \end{array}$$

i.e., for two contiguous vowels, if the second is stressed, the first vowel is stressed and the second loses its stress.

Where assimilation occurs, this format provides results that correspond to the notion that complete assimilation is more general than partial assimilation. A Southern Paiute rule that assimilates [h, ʔ] to a following consonant is:

$$\text{SD:} \quad \begin{bmatrix} -\text{cns} \\ -\text{voc} \end{bmatrix} \qquad [+\text{cns}]$$

(xxx)   1   2

$$\text{SC:} \quad 1 \longrightarrow 2$$

A rule for partial assimilation would require more features and Greek-letter variables.

In Modern German, [h] is best treated as the phonetic realization of an underlying velar fricative /x/. The rule that produces [h] must also make a reassignment of the compactness and graveness values from those of the compact, grave fricative to those of an immediately following vowel. Rule (xxxi) illustrates this:

$$\text{SD:} \quad + \begin{bmatrix} +\text{obs} \\ +\text{cnt} \\ +\text{grv} \\ +\text{cmp} \end{bmatrix} \qquad [+\text{syl}]$$

(xxxi)   1   2   3

$$\text{SC:} \quad 2 \longrightarrow \begin{bmatrix} 3 \\ -\text{syl} \\ -\text{vce} \end{bmatrix}$$

i.e., a velar fricative is assimilated to a following vowel, except that it is nonsyllabic (now becoming a glide) and voiceless.

The insertion of segments identical with some segment already present and metathesis can be handled easily by means of the above format.

Certain types of epenthesis, at a point below the rules that specify the redundant features of segments, can be handled in a very natural manner through the use of this format. For example, a rule that inserts [t d] segments into [ns nz] clusters would treat [t d] as a reduplication of [n] which is nonnasal and agrees in voicing with the following sibilant; thus,

$$\text{(xxxii)} \quad \text{SD:} \quad \begin{bmatrix} +\text{nas} \\ -\text{grv} \end{bmatrix} \quad \begin{bmatrix} +\text{obs} \\ +\text{cnt} \\ +\text{strid} \\ -\text{grv} \\ \alpha\text{vce} \end{bmatrix}$$

$$1 \qquad\qquad 2$$

$$\text{SC:} \quad 1 \longrightarrow 1 \quad \begin{bmatrix} 1 \\ -\text{nas} \\ \alpha\text{vce} \end{bmatrix}$$

This conforms well with the feeling that such insertions result from the extension of one of the two segments in addition to certain features carried over from the other segment.

12. A special convention has been proposed for handling certain situations in which there are certain exceptions to a general rule. One way to deal with such cases is first to apply the general rule and then to determine the desired output in the special cases by a later rule. For example, consider the somewhat simplified Southern Paiute stress rule above (xviii) that unstresses odd-numbered vowels. This presupposes a rule that has first redundantly stressed all vowels. A single rule can be constructed that comprehends rule (xviii) as well as the prior rule by adopting an 'alpha-environment' convention such that if the segment to the left of the arrow fits into the environment given to the right of the arrow, the value of alpha is 'plus'; otherwise, alpha is 'minus'. For this convention the entire environment is enclosed in angles preceded by an alpha; e.g.,

$$[\quad] \longrightarrow [\alpha F_i] \;/\; \alpha \langle \text{ab\_} \rangle$$

Thus the Southern Paiute stress rule can now be given as:

$$\text{(xxxiii)} \qquad V \longrightarrow [-\alpha\text{stress}] \;/\; \alpha \langle \; \ddagger \; (C_0 V C_0 V)_0 C_0 \text{\_} \rangle$$

i.e., odd-numbered vowels are unstressed (if alpha is 'plus', then stress is 'minus'), and even-numbered vowels are stressed.

Rule (vi) above can now be reduced to:

$$\text{(xxxiv)} \qquad [-\text{obs}] \longrightarrow [\alpha\text{nas}] \;/\; \alpha \left\langle \begin{bmatrix} +\text{cns} \\ -\text{voc} \end{bmatrix} \right\rangle$$

The possibility of using other Greek-letter variables within the environment, in the function of relating feature values, is not ruled out here; thus the following rule is possible in certain early Permic dialects, where central vowels are distinctively 'nonperipheral':

$$\text{(xxxv)} \qquad [\quad] \longrightarrow [\alpha\text{grv}] \;/\; \alpha \;\Big\langle\; \begin{bmatrix} \beta\overline{\text{perph}} \\ \beta\text{flt} \end{bmatrix} \;\Big\rangle$$

i.e., vowels for which peripheralness and rounding agree are grave; other vowels are nongrave.

Zürich German has a rule such as (xxxvi) which states that a low, front, rounded vowel becomes nonlow and nontense, and derives its flatness value from the following boundary and segmental environment (Becker, 1967). It is unrounded only before a [y] in the same morpheme; e.g., /kasy/ > [xɔ̈ : sy] > [xe : sy] > [xe : s] *cheese*, /sPạt┼yr/ > [špɔ̈ : t┼yr] > [špö : t┼yr] > [špö : tɾ] *later*.

$$\text{(xxxvi)} \quad \begin{bmatrix} +\text{syl} \\ +\text{cmp} \\ -\text{grv} \\ +\text{flt} \end{bmatrix} \longrightarrow \begin{bmatrix} -\text{cmp} \\ -\text{tns} \\ \alpha\text{flt} \end{bmatrix} \;/\; \alpha \;\Big\langle\; \underline{\qquad} \begin{bmatrix} -\text{syl} \\ \left\{\begin{matrix} +\text{cns} \\ +\text{grv} \end{matrix}\right\} \end{bmatrix}_0 + \;\Big\rangle$$

The environment here is 'before morpheme boundary with optional intervening consonants or [w]', thus excluding [y] in the same morpheme.

The alpha-environment convention is to be expanded as two conjunctively ordered subrules such that in the first subrule alpha is assigned a value of 'minus', and in the second subrule the value of alpha is switched to 'plus' in the environment enclosed in angles. Note the following rule for Umuoji Igbo (Bach, 1967):

$$\text{(xxxvii)} \quad \begin{bmatrix} +\text{voc} \\ -\text{cns} \\ -\text{grv} \\ -\text{high} \\ -\text{cmp} \end{bmatrix} \longrightarrow [\alpha\text{ tns}] \;/\; \alpha \;\Big\langle\; \underline{\qquad} C_0 \begin{bmatrix} +\text{voc} \\ -\text{cns} \\ +\text{tns} \end{bmatrix} \;\Big\rangle$$

which must be expanded, first to make all occurrences of the underlying tense, front, midvowel /e/ nontense [ε]; and then to switch [ε] back to [e] before an underlying tense vowel other than itself, e.g., /eCe/ > [εCε], /eCa/ > [εCa], /eCo/ > [εCo] > [eCo]. Without the above expansion convention, the tenseness of /e/ in /eCe/ would not be altered by the rule.

13. Closely related in function to the alpha-environment convention is the 'minus-next-rule' convention (cf. Ross, 1966; Chomsky and Halle, to appear). By this convention, segments are assigned a feature '−next rule' which prevents them from undergoing the immediately following rule, or rule expansion, of a conjunctively ordered abbreviation. Frequently, but not always, it is equivalent to the alpha-environment convention; thus, Rule (xxxiv) [= (vi)] above can be restated as:

$$(\text{xxxviii}) \quad [-\text{obs}] \longrightarrow \left\{ \begin{array}{l} \begin{bmatrix} +\text{nas} \\ -\text{next rule} \end{bmatrix} \Big/ \begin{bmatrix} \overline{+\text{cns}} \\ -\text{voc} \end{bmatrix} \\ [-\text{nas}] \end{array} \right\}$$

i.e., a nonobstruent that is nonvocalic and consonantal must be nasal, and does not undergo the next rule (here the second line of the braces), which specifies all other nonobstruents as nonnasal. Rule (xxxviii) differs from Rule (vi) solely in the feature '−next rule' and in the ordering of the subrules. If this '−next rule' is understood as a purely abbreviatory device, then it should not be counted in measuring the complexity of the rule; thus the choice between (vi) and (xxxviii) is arbitrary. In any case, Rule (xxxiv) provides a more economical statement of the generalization.

Consider, however, the following German rule (Ross, 1966) which cannot be treated in the manner of (vi) nor by the alpha-environment convention:

$$(\text{xxxix}) \quad \begin{bmatrix} V \\ +\text{cmp} \end{bmatrix} \longrightarrow \left\{ \begin{array}{l} [-\text{next rule}] \ / \ \_\_ \ [-\text{cns}] \\ \begin{bmatrix} -\text{dif} \\ +\text{grv} \\ -\text{flt} \end{bmatrix} \end{array} \right\}$$

i.e., the only low vowel is [a], except before a following glide or vowel, where both [ɔ] and [a] can occur. On the other hand, certain types of alpha-environment rules, such as (xxxvi), cannot be treated by the '−next rule' convention.

14. At times, special conditions may be imposed upon rules, where necessary, for the expression of desirable generalizations. Most fre-

quently these are constraints imposed upon the content of variables; e.g., Komi Jaźva has the stress rule:

(xl) $V \longrightarrow$ [+stress] / $\ddagger$ (X) _____

$$\text{Condition:}\quad \text{X does not contain} \begin{bmatrix} +\text{voc} \\ -\text{cns} \\ +\text{tns} \end{bmatrix}$$

i.e., stress falls only on the first tense vowel of the word, but if the word has only lax vowels, the final vowel is stressed; e.g., /śibdinǝ/ > [śibdinǝ́] *to bind*, /líććinǝ/ > [líććinǝ] *to descend*, /l'iśīnā/ > [l'iśína] *wood*. Note that both disjunctive order and the convention for expanding X-type variables are necessary for the application of this rule.

The following Southern Paiute rule imposes a condition upon alpha-type variables:

$$\text{(xli)}\qquad \begin{bmatrix} -\text{cns} \\ +\text{voc} \\ \alpha\text{grv} \\ \beta\text{cmp} \end{bmatrix} \longrightarrow [\alpha\text{flt}]$$

Condition: β is '+' or α is '−'.

i.e., graveness and flatness agree, except for vowels that are grave and noncompact. (The condition could also have been stated: 'if α is '+', then β is '+'.) In situations of this type, one of four possible '+' and '−' combinations is excluded by the condition.

Conditions may be placed upon angled parentheses such that an expansion with $\langle \ldots \rangle_i$ requires the presence of $\langle \ldots \rangle_j$, but not conversely, as is otherwise required in the unmarked case. Thus, certain Modern German dialects have a rule that, before a morpheme boundary or a vowel, shifts /p k/ to [f̄ x̄] after a vowel or liquid and /t/ to [s̄] after a vowel, (Becker, 1967).

$$\text{(xlii)}\qquad \begin{bmatrix} +\text{obs} \\ +\text{tns} \\ \langle -\text{grv}\rangle_a \end{bmatrix} \longrightarrow \begin{bmatrix} +\text{cnt} \\ +\text{strid} \end{bmatrix} / \begin{bmatrix} -\text{obs} \\ -\text{nas} \\ \langle -\text{cns}\rangle_b \end{bmatrix} \underline{\qquad} \left\{ \begin{matrix} + \\ [+\text{syl}] \end{matrix} \right\}$$

Condition: If a, then b.

The nongrave, tense obstruent /t/ undergoes the rule only after a nonnasal, nonobstruent segment which is also nonconsonantal, i.e., a vowel; but the other tense obstruents are altered after any nonnasal, nonobstruent segment.

The use of 'or' and 'if ... then' statements in conditions has been taken from modern logic, and can be understood in terms of tables corresponding to the 'truth tables' of logic. For example, the applicability of Rule (xli) above can be determined as follows:

value of αgrv	value of βcmp	condition is met (= rule applies)
−	+	yes
−	−	yes
+	+	yes
+	−	no

The applicability of Rule (xlii) requires the following type of table (assuming, apart from $\langle -grv\rangle_a$ and $\langle -cns\rangle_b$, that the structural description has been met):

$\langle -grv\rangle_a$ is present	$\langle -cns\rangle_b$ is present	$t > \bar{s}$	$p, k > \bar{f}, \bar{x}$
yes	yes	yes	—
yes	no	no	—
no	yes	—	yes
no	no	—	yes

Some of the above conventions still have bugs which must be worked out; e.g., the same general principle that led to the convention for deleting the environment bar also seems relevant to the following rule in a reconstructed stage of Udmurt:

$$(\text{xliii}) \quad \begin{bmatrix} +\text{voc} \\ -\text{cns} \\ +\text{buc} \\ -\text{cmp} \end{bmatrix} \longrightarrow [+\text{flt}] \ / \ \left\{ \begin{array}{l} \begin{bmatrix} +\text{cns} \\ +\text{grv} \\ -\text{high} \end{bmatrix} - \begin{bmatrix} +\text{cns} \\ -\text{shp} \end{bmatrix} \\ \begin{bmatrix} +\text{cns} \\ -\text{shp} \end{bmatrix} - \begin{bmatrix} +\text{cns} \\ +\text{grv} \\ -\text{high} \end{bmatrix} \end{array} \right\}$$

i.e., all midvowels are rounded in the immediate environment of a labial consonant unless also in the immediate environment of a palatalized consonant or /y/. Perhaps this environment is best abbreviated as:

$$/ \begin{bmatrix} +\text{cns} \\ +\text{grv} \\ -\text{high} \end{bmatrix}, \quad \begin{bmatrix} +\text{cns} \\ -\text{shp} \end{bmatrix}$$

Concerning the simplicity metric, in general the economy of each rule is determined by counting the *features* present in its unexpanded form. Arrows, parentheses, braces, numerals, and other special symbols are normally not counted. (Note that the number of *rules* involved is not a relevant factor in comparing two solutions, nor is the number of times a given rule will be used in the language.) Many of the above conventions raise problems concerning how things are to be counted if the simplicity metric is directly to reflect the relative generality of two rules. For example:

(a) Since [αflt] $\longrightarrow$ [αgrv] is more general than [−flt] $\longrightarrow$ [−grv], should alpha-type variables count less than the plus/minus values?
(b) Since the environment '/C' (after or before a C) is more general than '/__C', should the environment bar be assigned a value?
(c) Since the environment '__Xi' (=anywhere before [i]) is more general than '__i' (=immediately before [i]), should 'X' be assigned a negative value?
(d) $(CV)_0$ is more general than (CV), but how is the difference to be counted?

Given the above array of abbreviatory conventions, it is sometimes possible to arrive at equally simple results through the use of different devices. For example, (a) below expresses the same structural description as (b). The choice between them is apparently arbitrary.

(a) $\quad \begin{bmatrix} \left\{ \begin{matrix} +\text{dif} \\ +\text{cmp} \end{matrix} \right\} \end{bmatrix}$ (b) $\quad \begin{bmatrix} \alpha\text{dif} \\ -\alpha\text{cmp} \end{bmatrix}$

EXERCISES

1. The Mohawk rules below were presented in 1964 (Postal). How might they be reformulated under current abbreviatory conventions? (Use Postal's features.)

(a) MS2

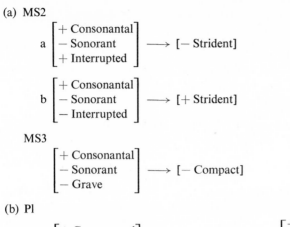

a $\begin{bmatrix} + \text{Consonantal} \\ - \text{Sonorant} \\ + \text{Interrupted} \end{bmatrix} \longrightarrow [- \text{Strident}]$

b $\begin{bmatrix} + \text{Consonantal} \\ - \text{Sonorant} \\ - \text{Interrupted} \end{bmatrix} \longrightarrow [+ \text{Strident}]$

MS3

$\begin{bmatrix} + \text{Consonantal} \\ - \text{Sonorant} \\ - \text{Grave} \end{bmatrix} \longrightarrow [- \text{Compact}]$

(b) Pl

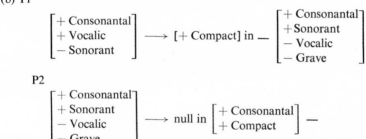

$\begin{bmatrix} + \text{Consonantal} \\ + \text{Vocalic} \\ - \text{Sonorant} \end{bmatrix} \longrightarrow [+ \text{Compact}] \text{ in } \_ \begin{bmatrix} + \text{Consonantal} \\ + \text{Sonorant} \\ - \text{Vocalic} \\ - \text{Grave} \end{bmatrix}$

P2

$\begin{bmatrix} + \text{Consonantal} \\ + \text{Sonorant} \\ - \text{Vocalic} \\ - \text{Grave} \end{bmatrix} \longrightarrow \text{null in } \begin{bmatrix} + \text{Consonantal} \\ + \text{Compact} \end{bmatrix} \_$

(The only consonantal segments not affected by Pl are /w y/.)

2. Construct rules to handle the phenomena described in the following statements:

   (a) In Warao, 'in polysyllabic words in which a series of vowels or vowels mixed with w, y, or h follows a nasal consonant or nasalized vowel, the vowels are all nasalized and nasalized allophones of w, y, h occur;' e.g., [inãw̃ãh̃ã] *summer*, [mõỹõ] *cormorant*, [mẽh̃õkohi] *shadow* (Osborn, 1966: 111). (Warao has no glottal stop phoneme.)

   (b) Diola-Fogny vowel harmony has been described in Exercise 2(a) of Chapter 4. Examples are (Sapir, 1965: 12–13): /ni-bay-ɛn-u/ > [nibayɛnu] *I caused you to have* (ni- *I*, -u *you* (pl.)), /ni-bay-ul̯-u/ > [nibəyul̯u] *I have for you*, /i-kik̯-i/ > [ik̯ik̯i] *I shave you* (sing.), /əi-aw/ > [əiəw] *the king*. Note further that all consonants are tense in the environment of tense vowels; elsewhere they are lax.

   (c) In Eastern Cheremis certain word final vowels are subject to vowel harmony such that:

1. If preceding vowels consist solely of [i e a ə], then the final vowel is [e];
2. If the vowel immediately preceding the final vowel, or separated from it only by [ə]'s, is [u o], then the final vowel is [o];
3. If the vowel immediately preceding the final vowel, or separated from it only by [ə]'s, is [ü ö], then the final vowel is [ö];
4. Nonfinally, the suffix vowel is [ə].

EXAMPLES: [βurɣemže] *his clothing*, [čoðrašte] *in the forest* (-šte 'loc.'), [kiðəštəže] *in his hand* (-že '3rd sing. poss.'), [βuyəšto] *in the head*, [βuyəštəžo] *in his head*, [pörtšö] *his house*, [tüŋəštö] *at the bottom*. What is the underlying form of the vowel? (Based on Sebeok and Ingemann, 1961.)

(d) In Eastern Cheremis, when vowels come together through affixation, the resultant clusters are reduced according to the following conditions:

1. If both vowels are identical, one is lost: /ača-at/ > [ačat] *father* (emphatic);
2. /ə/ is lost: /kornə-et/ > [kornet] *your way*;
3. /e/ is lost adjacent to /a/ : /ača-em/ > [ačam] *my father*;
4. Other clusters are retained: [pašueš] *in the field* (Sebeok and Ingemann, 1961).

(e) In Nootka, which has the three vowels /i o a/, the reduction of vowel clusters operates as follows (Mattingly, 1960: 82):

1. Any vowel is lost adjacent to /o/;
2. /a/ is lost adjacent to /i/;
3. If both vowels are identical, one is lost.

(f) Cocama devoicing is described in Exercise 5 of Chapter 5. Restate your answer to (c) in light of the abbreviatory conventions.

(g) In Finnish, the following assimilations take place across morpheme boundary:

1. l-n > ll : tul-nut > tullut *having come*
2. r-n > rr : pur-nut > purrut *having bitten*
3. s-n > ss : pes-nüt > pessüt *having washed*
4. t-n > nn : halut-nut > halunnut *having wanted*.

Other Finnish consonants are /p k h v m/.

(h) Eastern Cheremis stress is determined as follows (Sebeok and Ingemann, 1961: 9):

1. The final vowel is stressed, or optionally:

2. The next preceding vowel other than [ə] may be stressed; or, if only [ə]-vowels precede, then the first vowel of the word is stressed.

EXAMPLES: kitšə́m, kítšəm *his hand* (acc.)
šlapažə́m, šlapážəm *his hat* (acc.)
püγəlmö́, pǘγəlmö *cone*
kiðəštəžé, kíðəštəže *in his hand*
tələzə́n, tə́ləzən *moon* (gen.).

(i) The following conditions on stress exist in Egyptian Arabic (Harrell, 1957: 15):

1. The last syllable is stressed if the vowel is long or if the syllable is closed by two consonants; e.g., [katábt] *I wrote*, [sakakí : n] *knives.*
2. The antepenultimate vowel is stressed if the last three syllables comprise a CVCVCV(C) sequence and the preantepenultimate syllable is not CV, e.g., [búxala] *misers*, [ʔábadan] *never*; but [katabítu] *she wrote it* (masc.).
3. Elsewhere the penult is stressed, e.g., [yiktíbu] *they write*, [ɣamálti] *you* (fem. sing.) *did.* Do not allow more than one stress per word.

(j) In Diola-Fogny, if two consonants come together across morpheme boundary, the first is lost; if the preceding morpheme ends in a cluster, the whole cluster is lost, e.g., lɛt-ku-ġaw > lɛkuġaw *they won't go*, ɛ-rɛnt-rɛnt > ɛrɛrɛnt *it is light* (Sapir, 1965: 17). (Note that only two-consonant clusters occur within morphemes.)

(k) In Old Slavic an [l] was inserted between a labial consonant and [y], e.g., [lyubiti] *to love*, [lyublyõ] *I love*, [tvoriti] *to do*, [tvoryõ] *I do*, [zemlya] *earth*, [zemĭskŭ] *earthen.*

(l) Before a consonant or in word-final position, Hungarian roots in /r/ or /lʹ/ plus /h/ undergo metathesis and insert an [e] vowel between the /h/ and following liquid, e.g., /kelʹh-et/ [keyhet] *cup* (acc.) (/lʹ/ > [y]), /kelʹh-ben/ > [keheyben] *in the cup*, [teher] *burden*, [terhek] *burdens* Other Hungarian front short vowels are /i ü ö/.

(m) In Hausa, across morpheme boundary, underlying /w/ becomes [y] before [i e] (long and short), and /y/ becomes [w] before [o:], e.g., [ba : wà :] *slave*, [ba : yi :] *slaves*, [ya : sàya :] *he bought something*, [kàsawo : ši] *buy it* (*and bring it here*), [ma : yè :] *wizard*—but [ma : yu :] *wizards.* Hausa has the vowels /i i: e e: u u: o: a a:/. (Based on Hodge, 1947: 24–25.)

(n) In a closed syllable (before CC or C‡) Hausa /e:/ > [a]; /o:/ > [wa] after /k kʔ g d/ (other stops are /b bʔ t dʔ č čʔ/) and elsewhere /o:/ > [a]; and other vowels are shortened (Hodge, 1947: 26).

(o) In Cashinahua, between two unlike vowels, if the first vowel is one of /i u ʌ/, a glide is inserted such that:
1. After /i/, the glide is [y];
2. After /u/, the glide is [w];
3. After /ʌ/, the glide is [ɣ].

The only other vowel phoneme is /a/. /ʌ/ has 'freely fluctuating variants ranging from high back to midback position, with the norm for most informants being [ɨ]...' (Kensinger, 1963: 211–12). Give the rule for glide insertion only, but consider the choice of 'ʌ' as representing the nonlow central vowel.

3. The following assimilations of strident consonants are observed in Southern Paiute:

$$
\begin{array}{ll}
sV\check{s} > sVs & sV\check{c} > \check{s}V\check{c} \\
cV\check{s} > cVs & \check{c}Vs > \check{c}V\check{s} \\
cV\check{c} > \check{c}V\check{c} & \check{s}Vc > sVc
\end{array}
$$

(a) Formulate the rules necessary to handle the above changes and predict the results for: šVs, čVc.
(b) Can sequences of more than two stridents be assimilated by your rules (e.g., cVcVč, sVčVs, sVšVs)? Consider the role of the noniterative-rule convention.
(c) Compare your rules with Rules (vi) and (vii) in Chapter 6. What do these rules predict for (a)? Do they treat sequences of more than two stridents?
(d) Give rules in accord with the NIR convention that will predict the output of the underlying sequence čVsVs.

4. In Russian dialects of the Oboyan type, there are seven contrasting vowels under stress: [u e o ɛ ɔ a] and [i, ɨ] (where [ɨ] occurs after nonpalatalized consonants, [i] elsewhere). In the following examples, note the alternations in underlying root vowels after a palatalized consonant in the prestress syllable (based on Avanesov, 1949: 80–84).

śistrá	sister	ṕátnɨ	spots
śɔ́strɨ	sisters	ṕatnó	spot
śastrú	sister (acc.)	ṕitnóm	spot (instr.)
śastróy	sister (instr.)	visólay	gay
śastŕé	sister (prep.)	vɛ́sɪla	gaily
l'és	forest	ńasú	I carry
l'asnóy	forest (adj.)	ńɔ́s	(he) carried
l'isók	small wood	ńislá	(she) carried
		ńaśi	carry (sing.)!

(a) State the rule that operates on the prestress syllable. (*Note*: The rule does not affect high vowels.)

(b) Predict the results for underlying: [dɛrɛvńa] *village*, [pɔkl'í] *(they) baked*, [r̊eká] *river*.

5. Menomini is said to have the following conditions on the occurrence of vowel length which must be applied in the order given below (Bloomfield, 1939: 113–14):

1. In monosyllables all vowels are long: /pɛ?t-e/ > [pɛ̄?č] *by error*.

2. After two consonants and before a single consonant only short vowels occur: /kōhnɛw/ > [kōhnɛw] *he swallows him* (cf. [mɛ̄nɛ̄w] *he gives it to him*).

3. If the first two underlying vowels of a word are short, the second becomes long: /nɛ-pɛmāt-ɛse-m/ > [nepɛ̄mātɛsem] *I live* (cf. [pemātɛsew] *he lives*).

4. In an even-numbered syllable counting from the next preceding long vowel (i.e., any intervening vowels must be short), or from word boundary in words with an initial syllable in [V?] (again with only short vowels intervening):

    1. Only short vowels occur before a single consonant: /nōhtawɛ̄w/ > [nōhtawɛw] *he strikes him*, /pā-pɛm-e-ke-h-ɛ̄w/ > [pāpɛmekehɛw] *he brings him up*;

    2. Only long vowels occur before a consonant cluster: /kɛmew-an-ken/ > [kɛ̄mewāhken] *whenever it rains*.

    (a) Restate these conditions as feature rules.

    (b) Apply the rules to the underlying forms (note that nC > hC, t > č before e):

            /kɛ̄hken-ank-wā?/ *that which they know*
            /ko?t-ank-wā?/ *if they fear it*
            /ačet-e-kāpowe-h-ɛ̄w/ *he stands him upside down*

6. A Bravanese Swahili phrase (bounded by '|') may have at most one long vowel, which must occur either in the penultimate or in the antepenultimate syllable (cf. examples below). The vowels that are lengthened are, in part, lexically determined; thus, only the vowel of the first syllable of [ma : limu] can be long (cf. (d), where [a] is no longer antepenultimate). Any word-final vowel and any vowel before a nasal plus consonant sequence, can be long (e, h, i). A vowel before any other [CC] must be short. If a high vowel and another vowel occur in sequence, then the high vowel is lost (if [i] and [u], then [u] is lost), and the remaining vowel can be long (m). Certain suffixes, such as the locative, always add potential length to a preceding

vowel (j, o). The antepenultimate vowel is short if the penultimate syllable
has a potentially long vowel (in which case the penultimate vowel will be
long) or a vowel followed by a consonant cluster other than NC (compare
e-f-g, h-i-j, and k-l).

(a) xabari *news*
(b) ibu : ku *book*
(c) ma : limu *teacher*
(d) malimuwe *his teacher*
(e) malimu wa : saba *seventh teacher*
(f) malimu wa sitte *sixth teacher*
(g) malimu wa pi : li *second teacher*
(h) nu : mba *room*
(i) nu : mbaye *his house*
(j) numba : ni *in the house*
(k) ma : na *child*
(l) mana wi : tu *our child*
(m) ki : wa (<ku + iwa) *to know*
(n) mta : na *room*
(o) mtana : ni *in the room*

Give the rules that account for the above-vowel-length phenomena (do not
merely translate the above statements into rules but try to construct the
most reasonable overall system). Treat the locative suffix in a manner that
does not call for any extra rule machinery. (Based on Goodman, 1967.)

7. Consider the following statement describing Arabela /k/:

'The phoneme /k/ has allophones [k], [x], [g], and [γ]. The allophone
[k] occurs initial in the phonological phrase .... The other allophones
occur progressively and freely more lenis from [k] to [γ] as listed, within
the phonological phrase, due to a decrescendo of intensity over this
unit .... Stress can hinder the progress of this decay of intensity,
causing an interruption in the above order; that is, when a stressed
syllable occurs within the phonological phrase, a more fortis allophone
may occur after a more lenis one: [ˈkʌˈšæɣʌˈgwar: ˈtuʔ] /ˈka ˈšaka-
ˈkwarˈtu/ *pants*. The gradation of these allophones varies according to
the amount of decrescendo over a phonological phrase...and also
with different speakers.' (Rich, 1963: 194–95.)

Can the statement be translated into feature rules using the above devices?
How might it be treated?

8. The following rule has been invented for a hypothetical language:

$$[-\text{cmp}] \longrightarrow [-\alpha\text{flt}] \Big/ \left(\begin{cases} \left\{ \begin{matrix} + \\ [+\text{cmp}] \end{matrix} \right\} \\ \begin{bmatrix} -\text{cmp} \\ -\alpha\text{flt} \end{bmatrix} \end{cases} \right) [-\text{syl}] \begin{bmatrix} -\text{cmp} \\ \alpha\text{flt} \end{bmatrix} [\quad] —$$

i.e., noncompact vowels in a sequence of contiguous syllables cannot agree in rounding, and if the rounding of the underlying sequence of vowels is identical, all but the first noncompact vowel are dissimilated. (The upper limit of syllables in the word is three; all syllables consist of CV.) Thus, kokoko > kokëko, kikeko > kiköko > kikökë, kamɨkë > kamɨko.

(a) Does the rule conform to current abbreviatory conventions?

(b) Why was the upper limit on the number of syllables in a word stated?

(c) Consider the implications of your above answers in relation to a theory of natural language.

CHAPTER 8

Rule Components:
Morpheme Structure

Within the transformational model described by Chomsky in *Aspects of the Theory of Syntax*, phonological rules occur in two major components: 1. the morpheme structure component, and 2. the phonological, sometimes also 'morphophonemic' component.

Morpheme structure (MS) rules operate upon dictionary entries prior to the phonological (P) rules, and insert plus/minus feature-specifications for unspecified (redundant) features. These redundant lexical features lead to lexical economy, since they can be supplied by rules, and need not be listed in the individual segments of morphemes. The more economical dictionary, from a phonological point of view, is that which requires fewer features for the specifications of its morphemes

Two kinds of phonological redundancy are found in the listing of morphemes. One takes into consideration the limitations placed upon the occurrence of phonemes in linear sequence. A well-known example of this is the fact that for an English morpheme of the form CO ... (where O = obstruent), C has the features of [s], and that O is a voiceless stop (if it is a nonforeign word). Thus the first segment will require only one specified feature ([+cns] or [+obs]), and the second segment will not require features for continuance and voicing. Features which are otherwise distinctive for English /s/ and the stops can be supplied here by rules that utilize the limitations placed upon them by their segmental environment. These rules are known as *sequential constraint* rules.

A second type of rule specifies features that are nondistinctive in the language within any given segment, independent of surrounding segments; e.g., English obstruents, vowels, and semivowels are nonnasal; English nonobstruents are voiced. Rules of this type are commonly referred to as *blank-filling* rules.

The morpheme entry *spil* will, then, have a dictionary entry for its phonological form such as the following:

	s	p	i	l
cns	+	+	−	+
obs	θ	+	0	−
syl	0	0	+	0
nas	0	0	0	−
cnt	θ	θ	0	0
strid	θ	0	0	0
high	θ	−	+	0
grv	θ	+	−	0
flt	0	0	0	−
low	0	0	0	0
tns	0	0	−	0
vce	θ	θ	0	0

For purposes of illustration, two types of zeros have been indicated. Those zeros with an 'x' (θ) indicate features to be specified by sequential constraint rules; the other zeros will be specified by blank-filling rules Only the pluses and minuses are counted in determining lexical economy.

Sequential constraint rules describe many of the same phenomena traditionally treated by phonotactic statements. They differ, however, in several respects. First, phonotactic statements are generally presented as some kind of appendix to the phonemics, and the amount of phonotactic detail presented is generally left to the whim of the analyst. Here the MS rules are an essential part of the grammar, and the scope of the rules is clearly motivated by the feature savings which result. Second, a contrast is made here between those oppositions which serve to distinguish surface realizations of forms (words, utterances) and those which distinguish the underlying forms of morphemes. For example, in Russian final obstruents are voiceless: [rot] *genus* or *military company* (gen. pl.), but in other environments a voicing contrast is found: [rodə] *genus* (gen.), [rotə] *company*. The morphemes /rot/ and /rod/ must contrast in the voicing of final obstruents, final devoicing being determined by a late P rule and not by an MS rule.

In another sense the MS rules lie close to the traditional concern for canonic forms of morphemes (cf. Nida, 1949: 65–66), the motivation for which has never been very clearly stated. Within the framework of the MS component, once the canonical shapes of morphemes are determined, this can be utilized in the same manner as phonotactic contraints to effect a savings of features. For example, a language with a uniform CVCV ... morpheme structure would not have to specify consonantality and syllabicity for vowels, and for the consonant segments syllabicity could be omitted from the underlying representations; e.g.,

$$\text{(i)} \quad [\quad] \longrightarrow [\alpha\text{syl}] \;/\; \alpha \left\langle + [\quad] \left([\quad]_2^2\right)_0 - \right\rangle$$

i.e., even-numbered segments are syllabic and odd-numbered segments are nonsyllabic (where '+' indicates morpheme boundary):

$$\text{(ii)} \quad\quad\quad\quad\quad [+\text{syl}] \longrightarrow [-\text{cns}]$$

i.e., syllabic segments are vowels. Consonants would have to be distinctively specified as '−cns' for glides; or '+cns, +obs' for obstruents; or '+cns, −obs' for liquids and nasals.

Such factors naturally weigh heavily in making decisions whether a given phone or sequence of phones is to be analyzed as one phoneme or as a cluster. Consider, for example, the problem of [ts] and [pf] in German. The decision to treat them as unit phonemes leads to initial clusters consisting of: (a) obstruent plus resonant or /v/, and (b) /s/ plus stop (optionally followed by a liquid). A P rule will later provide [š] from /s/, thus making it possible to cover the inflectional morpheme /st/ > [st] '2 sing' by the same MS rule, e.g., /streik+st/ > [štreikst].

These very general constraints permit a considerable feature savings in the lexicon; e.g., an initial consonant before an obstruent is predictably [š] or [s]. The cluster solution for [ts], [pf], however, would substantially reduce the above savings. Since initial /tsv/ and /pfl/ would reduce the generality of rules concerning initial clusters, rule economy would also be adversely affected by the cluster solution.

The cluster versus unit question must also be considered from another point of view. The basic issue in problems of this type is whether to consider the property of affrication, nasalization (/Ṽ/ vs. /Vn/), aspiration (pʰ vs. /ph/), labialization (/kʷ/ vs. /kw/) as a feature within a segment or as a separate segment in a cluster. If the cluster solution is adopted, as frequently is the case with nasalized vowels, the lexical representation will require the features necessary for the given vowel or consonant (say, n features) in addition to the number of features required for the qualifying segment, such as /n, h, w, y/ (say, m features). Thus n-plus-m features are required for each such cluster. If the unit solution is adopted, as in the case of labiovelars in Southern Paiute (Harms, 1966a), the number of features required for each instance of a given vowel or consonant with the qualifying feature such as nasal, tense, flat, or sharp is n-plus-1 features; but, by the same token, each instance of the corresponding segment without the qualifying feature must be specified 'minus' for that feature (in accordance with the distinctiveness criterion) and will also count as n-plus-1 features. Thus the decision must be based upon the following type of comparison:

	unit solution	cluster solution
'qualified' phone or cluster	$n + 1$ features	$n + m$ features
simple phone	$n + 1$ features	n features
total	$2n + 2$ features	$2n + m$ features

The decision with regard to lexical economy can be made only after considering the value of m and the relative frequency of occurrence in the lexicon of the simple phone and the qualified phone or cluster. Consider, for example, the problem of aspirated stops in Bengali, where /h/ requires two features. Unaspirated stops are more frequent. If, for example, the dictionary contained 110 instances of nonaspirated stops and 100 instances of aspirated stops, the above schema would give the following results:

	unit solution	cluster solution
aspirated	$100n + 100$	$100n + 200$
nonaspirated	$110n + 110$	$110n$
total	$210n + 210$ features	$210n + 200$ features

Thus the cluster solution requires ten fewer features and would provide the more economical lexicon in this regard.

Since there is no necessary connection between MS rule economy of the type discussed above (for German affricates) and the second type (based upon relative frequency of occurrence, as in Bengali), conflicting results can arise. One apparent case of such conflict may be seen in Russian, where the MS rule generality favors the unit-phoneme treatment of palatalized consonants, supported further by P-rule generality, whereas the lexical feature-counting economy favors the cluster (/Cy/) approach (Harms, 1966b). T. Lightner's recent analysis of Russian (1963b, 1965a), however, obviates the need for underlying palatalized consonants, which are produced by rule before underlying front vowels and [y]. In such cases of conflict, the generality of the rules would seem more highly valued than savings in the listing of morphemes, but this creates a problem for the simplicity metric. Lexical feature savings are possible only through the addition of rules to the MS component. Why not, then, simply leave out certain complicated MS rules and just list those features as specified in the lexicon (a clearly undesirable approach)? Somehow the two approaches will have to be reconciled, but for the present, the key decisions can be made only on an intuitive basis.

Morpheme structure rules can account for the fact that native speakers of a language agree with great consistency on which of several nonoccurring forms could be admitted as new morphemes in their language; e.g., [stin] and [trin] for English, but not [θtin] (which conflicts with the MS constraint mentioned above) or [tlin] (since the only liquid that can follow an apical stop is /r/). But one should not always expect such a direct reflection of MS constraints in speaker reactions, especially where abstract underlying forms are not so apparently related to surface realizations.

The MS component will have to apply to those morphemes which are inserted via late transformational rules, as well as to lexical forms, e.g., inflectional and derivational affixes as well as certain function words such as English *to*, *not*, etc.

According to one point of view, MS rules can be characterized as feature-addition rules; P rules, as feature-switching rules. Although in general this relationship will hold true, it cannot be considered an absolute condition on the two components.

For maximum MS economy it will frequently prove desirable to switch features introduced by other MS rules; e.g., in English, stridence is redundant for all obstruents except /s z θ ð/. The most general specification of stridence for the remaining obstruents calls for a rule which first specifies all noncontinuant segments as nonstrident, and a second rule which specifies all high, nongrave (i.e., palatal) obstruents as strident:

(iii) $[-\text{cnt}] \longrightarrow [-\text{strid}]$

(iv) $\begin{bmatrix} -\text{grv} \\ +\text{high} \end{bmatrix} \longrightarrow [+\text{strid}]$

By Rule (iii), /č ǯ/ will become 'minus' strident, but by Rule (iv) they are switched to 'plus' strident, and at the same time /š ž/ become 'plus' strident. The condition on MS rules, then, would appear to be that they are allowed to switch only features that are redundant.

The Southern Paiute strident obstruents present an interesting situation, which, within one possible analysis, would further confound any attempt to equate the taxonomic phoneme with some unit or level in generative phonology. Consider the classificatory feature matrix for the Southern Paiute obstruents:

	t	č	š	p	k	kʷ
grv	−	−	−	+	+	+
strid	−	+	+			
cnt		−	+			
high				−	+	+
flt					−	+

Since the rule that determines the highness value of the [c č] allophones of /č/ (but not for /š/; cf. Chapter 6, Rule (vi) above) requires an environment that always belongs to the same morpheme as /č/, Rule (vi) in Chapter 6 could be treated as an MS rule, following Rule (v) below, which specifies /č š/ as redundantly '+high':

(v) $\begin{bmatrix} +\text{obs} \\ -\text{grv} \\ \alpha\text{strid} \end{bmatrix} \longrightarrow [\alpha\text{high}]$

Thus an MS rule could possibly correspond to traditional allophonic statements under the above circumstances. In this case, however, the lack of symmetry in setting up the above classificatory matrix will lead to an unmotivated loss of generality in the blank-filling rules, and one can question whether the [c č] allophones should be determined in the MS component, or, like the [s š] allophones, in the P rules (cf. Chapter 6, Rule (v)). On the other hand, Robert King has suggested sequential constraint MS rules for Modern German that predict the glides [w y] from underlying /u i/ and [s z] from /s/.

The output of the MS component has been the subject of some controversy. Must all feature-adding rules belong to the MS component (cf. McCawley, 1965)? If so, all segments upon which the P rules operate will be fully specified. Evidence in support of feature-adding P rules, however, is found in situations for which a P rule needed for switching feature values can also be used to specify sequential constraint redundancies. In Russian, for example, before /e/ the sharpness (palatalization) of consonants is predictable within morphemes, but the sharpness of morpheme-final consonants is distinctive; thus, in /1*et/ *summer* /1*/ is unspecified for sharpness, but /t/ is distinctively nonsharp (cf. /put'/ *path*. Inflectional forms in /e/, such as the prepositional suffix /e/, also call for the sharpness of a preceding consonant across morpheme boundaries; thus [l' et' e] *summer* (prep.). The same rule can serve the function of a sequential constraint rule to add the feature of sharpness in the /1*/ and switch the sharpness value of the final /t/ before an /e/ affix (cf. Halle, 1959: 63). Insistence upon all feature addition within the MS component would lead to two identical rules, one an MS rule, the other a P rule.

One minor notational problem arises in MS rules which must refer to initial or final position. Since the lexicon will not contain syntactic or morpheme boundaries (morpheme, word, or phrase junctures), a convention has generally been assumed which assigns a morpheme boundary before and after all morphs in the lexicon (cf. Halle, 1959: 58; McCawley, 1966: 7). Halle's MS rule that 'the segment after +RC is vocalic and nonconsonantal' ((1959: 58) could be expressed as:

$$\text{(vi)} \qquad [\quad] \longrightarrow \begin{bmatrix} +\text{voc} \\ -\text{cns} \end{bmatrix} \Big/ + \begin{bmatrix} +\text{voc} \\ +\text{cns} \end{bmatrix} \text{C}\underline{\quad}$$

A parenthesis might also serve the function of the above morpheme boundary; thus, the following Komi rule, which states that no initial consonant clusters occur:

(vii) $[\quad] \longrightarrow \begin{bmatrix} +\text{voc} \\ -\text{cns} \end{bmatrix} / (\ C\underline{\quad}$

McCawley employs MS rules of the following type for handling special classes of Japanese morphemes which are of Chinese origin, marked by the morpheme feature '+Sino' (McCawley, 1965: 126):

(viii) $[\quad] \longrightarrow \begin{bmatrix} -\text{cns} \\ +\text{voc} \end{bmatrix} / (\ [\quad]_{+\text{Sino}} \underline{\quad}$

i.e., the second segment in a Sino-Japanese morpheme is a vowel.

Finally, it should be noted that morpheme structure rules provide a kind of rigorous control against stating phonotactic generalizations that are actually circular. In Komi the following obstruent and resonant sequences are permitted:

OO
RR
RO

but not *OR.

Thus the following generalizations can be stated:

(ix) $[+\text{cns}] \longrightarrow [+\text{voc}] / \underline{\quad} \begin{bmatrix} +\text{cns} \\ +\text{voc} \end{bmatrix}$

i.e., if the second consonant of a CC cluster is a resonant, the first C must also be a resonant.

(x) $[+\text{cns}] \longrightarrow [-\text{voc}] / \begin{bmatrix} +\text{cns} \\ -\text{voc} \end{bmatrix} \underline{\quad}$

i.e., if the first consonant of a CC cluster is an obstruent, the second consonant must also be an obstruent. But both of these rules cannot be used, since, by the distinctiveness criterion, the application of either rule requires that the vocalicity of one segment already be specified. Thus it should be apparent that Rule (ix) assumes Rule (x), and vice versa. The existence of two independent generalizations here is only illusory.

EXERCISES

1. The distinctive features of Komi are:

	p	b	t	d	t′	d′	k	g	s	z	ć	ʒ́	ś	ź	č	ǯ	š	ž	m	n	ń	r	l	l′	y	i	ɨ	u	e	ə	o	a
cns	+	+	+	+	+	+	+	+	+	+	+	+	+	+	+	+	+	+	+	+	+	+	+	+	−	−	−	−	−	−	−	−
obs	+	+	+	+	+	+	+	+	+	+	+	+	+	+	+	+	+	+	−	−	−	−	−	−	−	+	+	+	+	+	+	+
syl																			+	+	+	−	−	−								
nas	−	−	−	−	−	−	−	−											+	+	+											
strid									+	+	+	+	+	+	+	+	+	+														
high	−	−	−	−	−	−	+	+	−	−	−	−	−	−	+	+	+	+								+	+	+	−	−	−	−
low																										−	−	+	−	−	+	
flt																										+	−	−	+	−	−	+
grv	+	+	−	−	−	−													+	−	−	+	−	−		−	+	−	+			
shp			−	−	+	+					−	−	+	+	+	+					−	+		−	+							
cnt									−	−	+	+	−	−	+	+																
vce	−	+	−	+	−	+	−	+	−	+	−	+	−	+																		

The following conditions upon phoneme sequences in Komi root morphemes may be stated:

1. No initial consonant clusters occur.
2. No initial vowel clusters occur. One apparent exception to this statement stems from the fact that initial [v] has been phonemicized as /u/, e.g., /uaž/ > [važ] *old*. In normal Komi words, [v] does not occur intervocalically; finally, or before a consonant, it is from underlying /l/; e.g., /uəl/ > [vəv] *horse* (cf. [vəlis] *the horse*).
3. The segment following a two-consonant cluster must be either [y] or a vowel.
4. Verbs other than (C)V- do not end in a vowel.
5. In a sequence CCy, the first C is [−obs], the second [+obs].
6. In a sequence of two consonantal segments, if the first is an obstruent, then the second is an obstruent.
7. In a sequence of two obstruents, if the first is strident, then both are voiceless and the second is a nonstrident stop other than /p/.
8. Beyond the first syllable, noun-final vowels are restricted to /i u a/; and of /i u/, /i/ occurs after palatalized consonants, /u/ elsewhere.
9. In a sequence of two nongrave consonants (except /y/), if the second is palatalized, then the first is also palatalized.

   (a) In light of the above data, provide the most economical phonological specification of the Komi roots: /kurćy/ *to bite*, /ošk/ *bear*, /uəl/ *horse*, /piśt′i/. Indicate feature savings that result from sequential constraints.

   (b) Formulate the sequential constraint rules and blank-filling rules that provide the fully specified morphemes. All rules must adhere to the distinctiveness criterion. Consider especially the /u/ plus vowel exception to Statement (2) above; i.e., should the rule take account of the apparent exception or should it provide a [w] 'allophone' of /u/. The blank-filling rules should specify all redundant features in the matrix above and not just those in the four roots.

(c) Give the four roots above as fully specified by your rules. Distinguish: 1. Those features which must be specified in the lexicon, 2. Those features which are supplied by sequential constraint rules, and 3. Those features supplied by blank-filling rules. Features added by rule should be keyed to the relevant rules, e.g.,

	b	o	ś	t	*to take*
cns	+	$\ominus^1$	+	+	
obs	+	$\boxminus^{11}$	+	$\oplus^6$	
syl	$\boxminus^{12}$	$\oplus^1$	$\boxminus^{12}$	$\boxminus^{12}$	

etc. . . .

where circled features are from sequential constraint rules, boxed features from blank rules, and raised numerals refer to the rules that supplied the given features.

(d) There is no morphophonemic u > v or w > v alternation. How is the additional rule complexity, necessitated by the treatment of [v] as phonemic /u/, to be justified?

2. The possibility of reanalyzing Komi /y/ as /i/ must also be considered. Note the following forms which illustrate the various conditions under which [y] and [i] occur in morphemes:

phonemicized as above	phonetic	
yi	yi	*ice*
yu	yu	*river*
uy	uy	*swim*
lïy	lïy	*shoot*
izy	izy	*stone*
yas	yas	*plural*
yay	yay	*meat*
uit	vit	*five*
uund	vund	*cut*
uïl	vïl	*upper surface*
yïl	yïl	*top*
uoy	voy	*night*
kuim	kuyim	*three*

(a) What changes in the MS rules of the above system would be necessitated? How might [kuyim] be phonemicized?

(b) Consider the relative economy of the two approaches with regard to feature specifications in the lexicon.

(c) Apart from economy, which approach provides a better description of the Komi phenomena?

3. Formulate the rules corresponding to the following constraints on phonemic sequences in morphemes in various languages, and illustrate the feature savings which the rules permit.

(a) Estonian has nine vowel phonemes /i u ü e o ö ə a ä/. Beyond the first syllable only /i e u o a/ occur in underlying forms. Vowel clusters occur only in initial syllables.

EXAMPLES: /ilo/ *beauty*, /oma/ *own*. ([ä] = [æ].)

(b) Finnish has the vowels /i e ü ö ä u o a/, which occur singly, as geminate clusters, and in certain mixed V^1V^2 clusters where V^2 is limited to /i ü u/ or the cluster is one of [ie], [üö], or [uo]. Morphophonemic evidence points toward treating these last three clusters as /ee/, /öö/, /oo/, respectively. Consider the implications of the proposed analysis; note that at the morpheme level, phonetic [e :], [ö :], [o :] occur only in loanwords or other special words.

EXAMPLES: /maa/ *land*, /tee/ *road*, /töö/ *work*, /puu/ *tree*, /koi/ *moth*, /pui/ *to thresh*, /siunat/ *to bless*.

(c) The 'vowel' harmony of Diola-Fogny has been presented in Exercise 2(a) of Chapter 4 and Exercise 2(b) of Chapter 7. The same constraints apply within morphemes. Will the MS rule be identical with the P rules? (Be careful to observe the distinctiveness criterion.)

(d) In Kolokuma Ịjọ, roots must contain only the close vowels /i e u o/ or only the open vowels /I ɛ U ɔ/, with the exception that /a/ can occur with either set of vowels, e.g., /éri/ *drying rack*, /ɛrI/ *see*, /ári/ *trick*, /árI/ *you* (sing.). Consider the desirability of setting up /a/ as two phonemes: /ʌ/ (close) and /a/ (open) in the underlying forms and a later rule by which ʌ > a.

Note further that morphophonemic vowel harmony in Kolokuma Ịjọ is restricted to prefixes and suffixes in a high vowel: [i-bo-mí] *I came*, [I-bɔ-mÍ] *I passed*, [u-dií] *look at him*, [U-tIÍn] *call him*; and a root with only [a]'s requires the open form of a high-vowel affix: [U-baá] *kill him*.

State all the rules relevant to the vowel harmony here. (Based on Williamson, 1965: 14–15.)

(e) In Cairo Arabic verb roots, if any given consonant is emphatic, then all preceding consonants are also emphatic.

(f) Cashinahua consonant-vowel sequences are free, with the following exceptions (Kensinger, 1963: 212):

1. /y/ does not occur before /i/.
2. /w/ does not occur before /i u/.
3. /ṣ/ does not occur before /i/.
4. /š/ does not occur before /ɨ/.
5. In the same syllable, /š/ does not follow /i/, and /š/ does not follow /ɨ/.
The phonemes are /p t c č k b d m n s š ṣ w y h i ɨ u a/.

(g) Glide plus vowel sequences in Arabela are limited to /y/ plus /a o u/ and /w/ plus /e a/ (Rich, 1963: 199). Arabela has the five vowels /i e a o u/.

CHAPTER 9

Rule Components: Phonological Rules

The phonological rules proper (P rules) operate upon segments in strings of morphemes in utterances supplied by the transformational component of the grammar. Rules requiring information from the syntactic components are applied first. Certain of the rules requiring syntactic information constitute a rule cycle which can be reapplied several times under stated conditions. Upon completion of the rule cycle, syntactic information is 'erased' from the string and is no longer available for lower rules. Phonological rules that do not apply in a cycle but that require syntactic information are called 'precycle' rules. Rules that follow the cycle are called 'postcycle' rules.

Cyclical rules require a syntactic bracketing of the utterance such as that provided by a tree diagram of a sentence. For example, the sentence *John wanted a cash discount* can be diagrammed as follows:

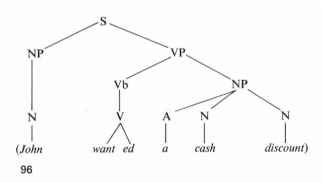

The information expressed in this tree diagram can also be expressed in terms of labeled brackets (numbered for easy reference in the discussion following):

```
4 2  1     1 2  3  2  1        1 2   2   1 1 1   1 1        1 2   3   4
[ [  [John] ]   [  [ [want + ed] ]  [  [a] [cash] [discount] ] ]   ]
S NP N     N NP VP Vb V        V Vb NP AA N    N N        N NP VP  S
```

The rules of the cycle are ordered, and each application of the cycle proceeds from the first rule to the last. Each application of the cycle operates only upon the smallest available constituents, i.e., applies only within the innermost brackets in the string (and not across a bracket). Upon the completion of a cycle, the innermost bracketing is 'erased' and the whole cycle is reapplied to the new set of smallest available constituents. This process is repeated until all bracketing is erased. In the above sentence the cycle will first apply to those forms within brackets with a raised '1'. These brackets will then be erased, providing the new string:

```
4 2    2    3   2         2   2              2   3   4
[ [John]   [  [want + ed]   [a + cash + discount] ]   ]
S NP    NP VP Vb        Vb NP              NP VP S
```

The second runthrough of the cycle will now apply to the morphs within the brackets with a raised '2', followed by erasure of these brackets.

This erasure procedure in effect removes nodes from the underlying syntactic structure until finally all constituents come directly from 'S' (which itself is finally lost). Thus, after four complete cycles, the string will have the form: + John + want + ed + a + cash + discount +

Rule cycles are known to account for a wide array of phonological phenomena in numerous languages, although it is too early to determine whether all languages employ this device. Syntactic stress in English and German, tone level in Igbo, vowel insertion in Komi, and certain segmental alternations in Russian (Halle, 1961, 1963; Lightner, 1965b) can be shown to require the use of cyclical rules.

English, for example, has, among others, the stress rule (based upon Chomsky and Miller, 1963):

$$(i) \quad V \longrightarrow [1 \ stress] \ / \ \begin{cases} [X\underline{\quad} \\ N \\ \underline{\quad}X] \\ NP \end{cases} \quad \begin{matrix} (a) \\ \\ (b) \end{matrix}$$

Condition: X does not contain (1 stress).

This rule operates upon *n*-ary numerical values for stress rather than upon plus/minus binary values. By universal convention, a rule that specifies a given vowel as '1 stress' also adds 'one' to the value of the previous stress values of all other vowels within the same brackets; i.e., any given [n stress] becomes [n + 1 stress] (where a higher numerical value indicates a weaker degree of stress). Rule (i) thus weakens all stresses in a sequence dominated by a noun (= N) and a noun phrase (= NP), except: (a) for the first (1 stress] in a noun, or (b) the last [1 stress] in a noun phrase.

Paul Kiparsky (1966) has proposed a somewhat modified version of this convention: If a vowel within a constituent receives the stress value *n*, then all other vowels in this constituent that also have the stress value *n* receive the value *n* + 1. The convention then applies iteratively as each stress value is successively altered; e.g., in the string 1-2-1-4, a rule that assigns [1 stress] to the initial member will (a) cause the second [1 stress] to become [2 stress], giving 1-*2-2-4, and, in turn, (b) replace the original [2 stress] with [3 stress], yielding finally 1-3-2-4. In contrast to the earlier convention, which would produce 1-3-2-5 here, the final [4 stress] will not shift further under Kiparsky's convention.

Applied to 'immediate cash discount', the above rule gives two results (depending upon the underlying syntactic structure): (a) Where it is a 'noun phrase,' in the sense of 'the discount was cash'; (b) Where it is a 'noun,' in the sense of 'the discount was given for immediate cash'. The rules that determine the word stress of 'immediate' are assumed to have already applied to it, but not to 'discount'; otherwise, all vowels are assigned a value of '1 stress'.

(a) Given:
$$\begin{array}{llllll} & ^3\ ^{1\ 32} & ^1 & ^{1\ 1} \\ [& [\text{immediate}] & [\text{cash}] & [\text{discount}] &] \\ \text{NP Adj} & \text{Adj N} & \text{N N} & \text{N NP} \end{array}$$

output of
1st cycle
(i)-a
$$\begin{array}{llllll} & ^3\ ^{1\ 32} & ^1 & ^{1\ 2} \\ [& [\text{immediate}] & [\text{cash}] & [\text{discount}] &] \\ \text{NP Adj} & \text{Adj N} & \text{N N} & \text{N NP} \end{array}$$

erase
brackets
$$\begin{array}{l} ^3\ ^{1\ 32}\quad ^1\quad ^{1\ 2} \\ [\text{immediate}{+}\text{cash}{+}\text{discount}] \\ \text{NP}\qquad\qquad\qquad\qquad \text{NP} \end{array}$$

output of
2nd cycle
(i)-b
$$\begin{array}{l} ^4\quad ^{2\ 43}\quad ^2\quad ^{1\ 3} \\ [\text{immediate}{+}\text{cash}{+}\text{discount}] \\ \text{NP}\qquad\qquad\qquad\qquad \text{NP} \end{array}$$

erase
brackets
$$\begin{array}{l} ^4\quad ^{2\ 43}\quad ^2\quad ^{1\ 3} \\ \text{immediate}{+}\text{cash}{+}\text{discount} \end{array}$$

b) Given:

$$\begin{array}{c} {}^3 \quad {}^1 \;\; {}^{32} \quad {}^1 \qquad\qquad {}^1 \;\; {}^1 \\ [\;\;[\;\;\; [\text{immediate}]\;\;[\text{cash}] \qquad\quad]\;[\text{discount}]\;\;] \\ \text{N NP Adj}\qquad\quad \text{Adj N}\quad\text{N NP N}\qquad\quad \text{N N} \end{array}$$

output of
1st cycle
(i)-a

$$\begin{array}{c} {}^3 \quad {}^1 \;\; {}^{32} \quad {}^1 \qquad\qquad {}^1 \;\; {}^2 \\ [\;\;[\;\;\; [\text{immediate}]\;\;[\text{cash}] \qquad\quad]\;[\text{discount}]\;\;] \\ \text{N NP Adj}\qquad\quad \text{Adj N}\quad\text{N NP N}\qquad\quad \text{N N} \end{array}$$

erase
brackets

$$\begin{array}{c} {}^3 \quad\;\; {}^1 \;\; {}^{32} \;\; {}^1 \qquad {}^1 \;\; {}^2 \\ [\;\;[\text{immediate}{+}\text{cash}]\;\;\text{discount}] \\ \text{N NP}\qquad\qquad \text{NP}\qquad\quad \text{N} \end{array}$$

output of
2nd cycle
(i)-b

$$\begin{array}{c} {}^4 \quad\;\; {}^2 \;\; {}^{43} \;\; {}^1 \qquad {}^1 \;\; {}^2 \\ [\;\;[\text{immediate}{+}\text{cash}]\;\;\text{discount}] \\ \text{N NP}\qquad\qquad \text{NP}\qquad\quad \text{N} \end{array}$$

erase
brackets

$$\begin{array}{c} {}^4 \quad\;\; {}^2 \;\; {}^{43} \;\; {}^1 \quad\; {}^1 \;\; {}^2 \\ [\text{immediate}{+}\text{cash}{+}\text{discount}] \\ \text{N}\qquad\qquad\qquad\qquad \text{N} \end{array}$$

output of
3rd cycle
(i)-a

$$\begin{array}{c} {}^5 \quad\;\; {}^3 \;\; {}^{54} \;\; {}^1 \quad\; {}^2 \;\; {}^3 \\ [\text{immediate}{+}\text{cash}{+}\text{discount}] \\ \text{N}\qquad\qquad\qquad\qquad \text{N} \end{array}$$

erase
brackets

$$\begin{array}{c} {}^5 \quad\;\; {}^3 \;\; {}^{54} \;\; {}^1 \quad\; {}^2 \;\; {}^3 \\ \text{immediate}{+}\text{cash}{+}\text{discount} \end{array}$$

Komi has the vowel insertion rule (ii) for breaking up certain three-consonant clusters which must be applied as a cyclical rule. The rule accounts for certain troublesome allomorphic alternations involving the presence or absence of [ɨ]: [vundinɨ] *to cut*, [bərdnɨ] *to cry*, [vundiśnɨ] *to cut oneself*, [pukśinɨ] *to sit down* (-ś- reflexive) : [bərd'ʒinɨ] (< [bər-dźinɨ]) *to begin to cry* (-ź- *begin*), [śetlinɨ] *to give for a time*, [ćet'ćivnɨ] (< [ćećyilnɨ]) *to get up for a time*.

$$(ii) \qquad \text{null} \longrightarrow \begin{bmatrix} +\text{voc} \\ -\text{cns} \\ +\text{high} \\ +\text{grv} \\ -\text{flt} \end{bmatrix} \; / \; \left\{ \begin{array}{c} C \begin{bmatrix} \alpha\text{voc} \\ \alpha\text{cns} \end{bmatrix} \\[2mm] \begin{bmatrix} \begin{bmatrix} +\text{obs} \\ +\text{nas} \end{bmatrix} \end{bmatrix} \; [+\text{obs}] \end{array} \right\} + \underline{\quad} C$$

i.e., [ɨ] is inserted before a consonant following (a) a consonant plus a semivowel or resonant, or (b) an obstruent after an obstruent or nasal. The presence of the morpheme boundary (+) in the environment is used to assign the added vowel to the following morpheme. The examples below illustrate the need for the rule's cyclical application:

Given:	[[puk+ś] ni]	[[ćećy+l] ni]	[[vund+ś] ni]
	Inf V V Inf	Inf V V Inf	Inf V V Inf
after			
first	[puk+ś+ni]	[ćećy+il+ni]	[vund+iś+ni]
cycle	Inf Inf	Inf Inf	Inf Inf
after			
second	puk+ś+ini	ćećy+il+ni	vund+iś+ni
cycle			

With /ćećy+1+ni/ and /vund+ś+ni/ a cyclical application is imperative. Since both the sequences [ćy-l], [nd-s] and [yl-n], [dś-n] meet the structural description of Rule (ii), the order of application in these cases would be ambiguous, and the correct results could not be determined without substantial further complication of the rule.   Since the successful application of the cyclical rules requires the erasure of the underlying syntactic structure, any noncyclical rules that require such information must be treated as precycle rules. The following rule from Igbo determines the echo-tone value in nouns with an uninterrupted sequence of [+high] tones when such nouns function as the subject of the sentence (i.e., stand immediately before a Predicate Phrase constituent; Carrell, 1966). (The tones are treated as syllable features.)

(iii) $[+high] \longrightarrow [+echo] \ / \ X \ [+high]_1 \_ Y_N^{\}} \ \hat{} \ PredP$

The first high tone syllable in the noun retains its [−echo] value, but following high tone syllables are '+echo'; e.g., [ósísí] *tree*, with all [+high, −echo] tones, in subject function, will alter both [í]'s to [+echo].

Either parentheses or brackets may be used to indicate syntactic constituent structure, but the interpretation of such parentheses or brackets is in no sense related to the conventions for abbreviatory devices. A left (or right) syntactic parenthesis or bracket indicates the leftmost (or rightmost) boundary of the given constituent.

Phonological rules that do not require syntactic information and that do not belong to the rule cycle are considered to be postcycle rules. These rules will account for all other 'morphophonemic' alternations and supply any remaining phonetic detail necessary for the realization of utterances.

In low-level P rules many features will eventually be converted to an *n*-ary value system. Numerous rules posited by James Sledd in his work on Southern dialects (1966) are essentially of this nature; e.g., 'Vowels and diphthongs are somewhat shortened before voiceless consonants' (37); 'medial consonants and liquids move toward the clear or dark ends of the scale according as they stand before the front or back reduction vowel (!ɪ! or !ə!)' (37). McCawley labels such distinctions as 'subfeatural': 'The phonetic difference between them would appear only in the "feature interpretation rules" which convert the feature specifications into ranges of physical variables' (McCawley, 1965: 83–84).

The details concerning just how these subfeatural distinctions are to be treated remain to be worked out. One possible approach might be to retain the plus/minus specifications together with the n-ary features. Each feature could then be assumed by general convention to contain a three-member $\alpha\widehat{\ }n\widehat{\ }F_i$ representation, i.e., plus/minus value, n-ary value, and the given feature. n would be assumed to have a value of '1' for all features until altered by low-level rules; thus $[\alpha\ grv] = [\alpha\ 1\ grv]$. A scale for graveness could be set up such that a higher graveness value indicated a more 'peripheral' articulation of consonants or a more back articulation of vowels. Bilabial consonants would thus be $[+\ 2\ grv]$; labiodentals, $[+\ 1\ grv]$. Rule (iv), for example, specifies all labial stops (including nasals) as bilabial:

$$(\text{iv}) \qquad \begin{bmatrix} +\,\text{grv} \\ -\,\text{high} \\ -\,\text{cnt} \end{bmatrix} \longrightarrow [2\ \text{grv}]$$

Note that both binary and n-ary values are employed in the same rule—the convention here being that only those values which are directly relevant to the rule will be given. Rule (iv) is probably a substantive universal and would not be counted in determining the complexity of any given phonology.

Swahili has back velar stop variants before grave vowels and front variants before front vowels (Harris, 1951: 122). Since Swahili already contrasts four series of stops in graveness and highness (p : t : č : k), some other means, such as rule (v), must be found for treating the [k] : [k̰] distinction.

$$(\text{v}) \qquad \begin{bmatrix} +\,\text{obs} \\ -\,\text{cnt} \\ +\,\text{grv} \\ +\,\text{high} \end{bmatrix} \longrightarrow [2\ \text{high}] \ / \ — \ \begin{bmatrix} +\,\text{syl} \\ +\,\text{grv} \end{bmatrix}$$

i.e., back velar stops are [+2 high]; front velars, [+1 high], where for consonants a higher value for highness indicates a position further removed from the point of division between high and nonhigh.

In Swahili, nasals assimilate to a following labiodental obstruent. To handle this, a variable indicating agreement of numerical value can be employed. Thus Rule (vi) would follow (iv) above and the nasal-assimilation Rule (xii) of Chapter 6.

$$\text{(vi)} \qquad [+\text{nas}] \longrightarrow [n\ \text{grv}]\ /\ \underline{\quad} \begin{bmatrix} +\text{cns} \\ -\text{high} \\ +n\ \text{grv} \end{bmatrix}$$

e.g., [m] will become [ɱ] ('1 grv') before [v, f], but elsewhere will remain '2 grv'. In this regard it should be noted that with the original Jakobsonian features, bilabial and labiodental fricatives can be contrasted in stridence, but no means is provided for contrasting two kinds of labial nasals or stops. This amounts to a hypothesis, apparently valid, that no language will contrast such sounds at the systematic phonemic level. McCawley's suggested feature of retracted articulation can handle all the above contrasts, but the universal limitations on the phonemic use of these contrasts must then be stated separately.

Phonological rules contribute directly to lexical economy. Perhaps the single most important guideline for analytical procedure is that all variants (allomorphs) of any given morpheme will be derived from a single underlying base form (except in cases of suppletion). This procedural assumption interacting with the simplicity metric should lead to the discovery of the most general phonological processes of the language, and, at the same time, make possible a lexicon with a minimum number of special instances of allomorphic variation. Consider, for example, the following Russian words: [xólət] *the cold*, [xəlʌdá] [*wintry*] *cold* (pl.), [xʌlódnəy] *cold* (adj.). All variants of the morpheme *cold* can be derived from a single underlying form /xolod/ in accordance with very general rules.

In a similar manner, the following Tonkawa words can be derived from a single set of base forms by general rules: (a) [yakpoʔ] *he hits him*, (b) [keykapoʔ] *he hits me*, (c) [yakakpoʔ] *he hits him repeatedly*— the morpheme *hit* in all these cases has the underlying form /yakap/ (cf. Hoijer, 1946). The reduplication in (c), however, will require the use of a morpheme feature (cf. Chapter 10). Not all such rules will be equally general. Indeed, some will apply only to a single morpheme; e.g., the

Finnish past participle form /nut/, followed by an [e], deletes its [t] via a general rule, but the subsequent assimilation of [u] to [e] is applicable only to this morpheme: /saa+nut+e+t/ > [saa+nu+e+t] > [saaneet] *received*, but /olut+e+t/ > [oluet] *beers*. Suppletion is reserved for those cases in which the selection of an entire morph must be made on a nonphonological basis, e.g., Finnish /hyvä/ and /parah/ (comparative and superlative) *good*; Estonian /min/ and /läkt/ *go*.

The treatment of certain intermediate cases is often unclear in this respect. In Finnish the impersonal morpheme /ta/ and the past participle /nut/ partially fuse to give the portmanteau [tu], where the initial [t] in both /ta/ and [tu] has certain morphophonemic peculiarities that require the use of a morpheme feature [+impersonal]. One approach would be to treat this fusion as a phonological process, as in the precycle Rule (vii).

(vii)   SD: ta)   +nut
                     [+impers]
                     12   345
               SC: 2, 3, 5 ⟶ null

Another approach would be to use the morpheme features that lead to the insertion of the above forms in such a manner that a verb that has the features '+impersonal, +past, +participle' will insert /tu/ directly. e.g.,

(viii)   SD: [+V, +impers, +past, +part]
                              1
              SC: 1 ⟶ 1 ⌢ tu

The second solution is more attractive, since the ad-hoc changes brought about by Rule (vii) do not seem to be phonological in nature.

EXERCISES

1. State the rules that treat the following Yoruba phenomena (Bamgboṣe, 1965):
   (a) In a noun plus noun sequence, an initial /i/ vowel of the second noun is assimilated to the final vowel of the first noun:
      > ará ìlú > aráàlú *townsmen*
      > ɛrù igi > ɛrùugi *bundle of wood*
   (b) In a verb plus noun sequence, where the verb ends in a vowel and the noun begins with a vowel:

1. /i/ (of verb or noun) is deleted:

> wo ilè > wolè *look at the ground*
> yí asɔ > yásɔ *steal clothes*

2. except before /i/, /u/ is lost:

> yu igi > yugi *throw a stick*
> bu omi > bomi *take water*

2. Halle (1963) sets up the following rules for Russian:
   (a) A vowel immediately following a morpheme-final stressed vowel is stressed.
   (b) A morpheme-final vowel is lost immediately before a morpheme beginning with a vowel.
   (c) Certain consonants are palatalized before a vowel after which stands a morpheme beginning with a rounded vowel; thus:

> t, k > č
> d, g, z, > ž
> s, x > š
> labial C > labial C plus [l′]
> l > l′

Applied to the appropriate underlying forms, the rules provide:

> ((brós+i+i)+u) >> bróšu *I shall throw*
> ((pis+á+o)+u) >> pišú *I write*

1. Restate the rules as feature rules.
2. Determine the order and manner of application of the rules.

3. Cocama stress may be described as follows (Faust and Pike, 1959: 22):
   (a) Primary stress occurs on the final vowel of words ending in a consonant; otherwise on the penultimate vowel: [amáska] *reaches*, [amaskán] *that which reaches*, [kakíri] *lives*, [kakirín] *alive*.
   (b) Secondary stress occurs on every other syllable, counting from the primary stress to the beginning of the word: [wàcarìpamái] *harlot*, [čipìtawára] *the one who pays*.

State the appropriate rules.

4. Komi Ižma:

1. munni	*to go*		9. liyi	*I shot*
2. muni	*I went*		10. kɨ : ni	*to hear*
3. voni	*to arrive*		11. kɨli	*I heard*
4. voyi	*I arrived*		12. po : ni	*to fear*
5. voa	*I arrive*		13. pola	*I fear*
6. loni	*to become*		14. lebni	*to fly*
7. loyi	*I became*		15. lebɔ	*flies*
8. liyni	*to shoot*		16. lebo : ni	*to fly* (indef.)

17. lebalə	*flies* (indef.)	24. sutni	*to stand up*
18. pirni	*to drop in*	25. və :	*horse*
19. pirtni	*to carry in*	26. və : li	*to a horse*
20. sulo : ni	*to stand*	27. vəlis	*the horse*
21. sulali	*I stood*	28. pi :	*cloud*
22. su : to : ni	*to stand up*	29. pilis	*the cloud*
	(repeatedly)	30. pi	*son*
23. su : tali	*I stood up*	31. pili	*to a son*
	(repeatedly)	32. piyis	*the son*

(a) Does the minimal pair [pi] : [pi :] demonstrate the existence of phonemic vowel length?

(b) Give the underlying forms for those words which differ from their systematic phonemic shape. State the rules that provide the phonetic forms.

(c) The only instance of long [e :] was in the undeclined adverb [ze :] *very*. What is its underlying form?

5. Compare the following sets of Estonian words (where [.] = syllable boundary, [:] = one additional mora of length on the preceding segment, stress always on the initial syllable):

    (a) li.na   *flax*
           lin.na   *city* (gen.)
           lin :.na   *city* (partitive)
    (b) sa.Da   *one hundred*
           sa :.Da   *send!*
           sa : :.Da   *to get*
    (c) kənet   *speeches*
           kənet :   *speech* (part.)
    (d) kań : :   *toy*
           kan : :   *jug*
    (e) kaś : t   *box*
           mus : t   *black*
    (f) mat' : :   *mat*
           vet : :   *water* (part.)

What types of phonological claims concerning Estonian quantity and palatalization appear to be supported by the above data? Consider further, however, the following paradigms:

	city	*toy*	*jug*	*box*	*black*
nom.	lin : :	kań : :	kan : :	kaś : t	mus : t
gen.	linna	kańni	kannu	kaśti	musta
part.	lin : na	kań : ni	kan : nu	kaś : ti	mus : ta
iness.	linnas	kańnis	kannus	kaśtis	mustas

	mat	*haste*	*birch*	*knee*	*belief*
nom.	mat′ : :	rut : :	kaś : k	pəl′ : v	us : k
gen.	mat′ti	ruttu	kase	pəlve	usu
part.	mat′ : ti	rut : tu	kas : ke	pəl : ve	us : ku

	leech	*hay*	*ship*	*apple*	*mercy*
nom.	ka : : ń	hei : n	lae : v	əu : n	ar : m
gen.	ka : ńi	heina	laeva	əuna	armu
part.	ka : : ńi	hei : na	lae : va	əu : na	ar : mu

	water	*hand*	*snow*	*river*	*land*
nom.	veśi	käśi	lumi	yəGi	ma : :
gen.	ve : :	käe :	lume	yəe :	ma : :
part.	vet : :	kät : :	lun : ᴅ	yəGe	ma : : ᴅ

	dark	*fine*	*heart*	*place*
nom.	pime	tore	süᴅa	ase
gen.	pimeᴅa	toreᴅa	süᴅame	aseme
iness.	pimeᴅas	toreᴅas	süᴅames	asemes

The partitives of se- *this*, ke- *who*, are [seᴅa], [keᴅa]. *Note also*:

1. Palatalized apical consonants occur immediately following an initial-syllable vowel where the vowel of the second syllable is [i], or in the nominative of stems that in the genitive have an [i] or an [e]—except for certain e-stems; cf. [ho : : l′] *care*: [ho : le] (gen.), but [tu : : l] *wind*: [tu : le]

2. The gen. sing. stem is generally identical with the stem form of the nominative plural, marked by /t/, e.g., [linnat], [kaśtit], [kaset], [ve : : ᴅ], [lumet], [ma : : ᴅ], [pimeᴅat].

3. Certain nouns, such as *hand*, *water*, *snow*, add the partitive to a consonant stem form, but in the nominative and genitive have the stem vowels [i] and [e]. Other nouns such as *new* behave as follows: nom. [u : : s], gen. [u : e], part. [u : : t :].

4. The following forms are normally not permitted as citation forms: CV :, CVC, CVCC, CV : C.

5. Beyond the initial syllable, only short vowels occur, and [C : C] or [C : :] sequences are not permitted.

6. Within a sentence, if the word does not receive a sentence stress, the extra length does not occur, e.g., [linna] *city* (part. or gen.), [heina] *hay* (part. or gen.), [usku] *belief* (part.), [ve :] *water* (gen.).

(a) In light of the above data, evaluate the following claims:
1. Estonian has the apical phonemes /t s n l r t′ s′ n′ l′/.
2. Estonian has three phonemic degrees of vowel length and three phonemic degrees of consonant length.
3. Estonian long vowels are best phonemicized as geminate clusters, e.g., [a :] = /aa/, [a : :] = /aa/, plus some marker of extra length.
4. Estonian long consonants are best phonemicized as geminate clusters.
5. The nominative, genitive, and partitive singular of the noun types illustrated above show stem suppletion, the case endings in question being different kinds of 'zero'; e.g., $-\emptyset_n$, $-\emptyset_g$, $-\emptyset_p$.
(b) Propose a set of underlying forms and rules that account for the noun paradigms given above. State the feature matrix that your analysis presupposes.

6. (a) Estonian has the nine vowels /i ü u e ö o ə ä a/. Other than the first vowel of a word, except as the second vowel of a geminate cluster, only five vowels occur, [i e u o a], and phonetic [o] never occurs beyond the first syllable.

Consider the following nominative and illative ('into') forms (ignoring extra quantity):

	head	land	mouth	night	swamp
nom.	pää	maa	suu	öö	soo
ill.	pähe	maha	suhu	öhe	sohu

Note: The sequence *[VVhV] does not occur in Estonian.

1. Posit underlying strings for the illative forms and give the rules for determining the correct phonetic output. (Make explicit the feature matrix for the vowels.)
2. Certain dialects differ from the above in one respect: the nom. of *head* is [pea] via a general rule by which [ää] becomes [ea]. Formulate the rules needed for such dialects.

(b) Consider, also, the following paradigms:

	story	snake	room	row	ceiling
nom.	luɢu	maᴅu	tuʙa	riᴅa	laɢi
gen.	loo	mao	toa	rea	lae
part.	luɢu	maᴅu	tuʙa	riᴅa	laɢe

	mountain	*sister*	*support*	*breakup*
nom.	mäGi	әɒe	tuGi	laGu
gen.	mäe	әe	toe	lao
part.	mäGe	әɒe	tuGe	laGu

	true	*hand*	*water*	*wolf*	*coal*
nom.	tәśi	käśi	veśi	suśi	süśi
gen.	tәe	käe	vee	soe	söe
part.	tәtt	kätt	vett	sutt	sütt

Compare the following forms: [puu] *tree*, [au] *honor*, [koi] *moth*, [lәuG] *jaw*, [kius] *spite*, [maiɒ] *lands* (part.), [puiɒ] *trees* (part.). Take into consideration the data presented in the preceding Estonian exercises and the general constraints on vowel occurrences presented above.

1. Posit underlying forms for the above paradigms and give rules that provide the given output; the rules should not lead to undesirable consequences in the other forms cited above.
2. Are any of the rules used for (a) needed to treat the data of (b)?

7. Determine the underlying forms of the Eastern Ojibwa morphemes in the following words and the rules for their phonetic realization (based on Bloomfield, 1957).

1.	ko : kko : šš	*pig*
2.	ko : kko : ššak	*pigs*
3.	ko : kko : ššan	*pig(s)*
4.	nenko : kko : ššim	*my pig*
5.	keko : kko : ššim	*thy pig*
6.	uko : kko : ššeman	*his pig(s)*
7.	nenko : kko : ššemina : n	*our pig*
8.	keko : kko : ššemina : n	*our pig*
9.	keko : kko : ššemina : nak	*our pigs*
10.	uko : kko : ššeminuwan	*the other's pig(s)*
11.	keko : kko : ššemiwa :	*your pig*
12.	keko : kko : ššemiwa : k	*your pigs*
13.	uko : kko : ššemiwa : n	*their pig(s)*
14.	uko : kko : ššemini	*the other's pig*
15.	ukima :	*chief*
16.	ukima : k	*chiefs*
17.	ukima : n	*chief(s)*
18.	nento : kema : m	*my chief*
19.	keto : kema : m	*thy chief*
20.	nento : kema : mena : n	*our chief*

21. keto : kema : muwa :   *your chief*
22. uto : kema : man   *his chief(s)*
23. uto : kema : muwa : n   *their chief(s)*
24. keto : kema : mena : n   *our chief*
25. šeka : k   *skunk*
26. šeka : kok   *skunks*
27. šeka : kon   *skunk(s)*
28. nešika : kom   *my skunk*
29. nešika : kumina : n   *our skunk*
30. kešika : kumiwa :   *your skunk*
31. ušika : kuman   *his skunk(s)*
32. uppin   *potato*
33. nento : ppeni : mak   *my potatoes*
34. mettik   *wood*
35. kemittekom   *thy stick*
36. umittekomuwa : n   *their stick(s)*
37. mekkisin   *moccasin*
38. mekkisenan   *moccasins*
39. umakkesin   *his moccasin*
40. umakkesinan   *his moccasins*
41. nemakkesinena : n   *our moccasin*
42. kemakkesinena : nink   *in our moccasin*
43. kemakkesinuwa : nk   *in your moccasin*
44. wi : kuwa : m   *house*
45. nuwi : kuwa : m   *my house*
46. kuwi : kuwa : mink   *in thy house*
47. uwi : kuwa : muwa :   *their house*
48. uwi : kuwa : muwa : nk   *in their house*
49. epwi   *paddle*
50. epwi : n   *paddles*
51. nentapwi   *my paddle*
52. utapwi : wa :   *their paddle*
53. epwi : nk   *on the paddle*
54. ci : ma : n   *canoe*
55. ci : ma : nink   *in the canoe*
56. nenci : ma : nink   *in my canoe*
57. ekkikk   *kettle*
58. ekkikko : n   *kettles*
59. ekkikkonk   *in the kettle*
60. ketakkekkona : nink   *in our kettle*

CHAPTER 10

Junctures, Syllables, and Morpheme Features

A. Junctures. Rules and examples in the preceding sections contained various boundary symbols, primarily morpheme boundary '╪' and word boundary '╪'. Rules such as (ii) in Chapter 9, however, can not be fully understood without further discussion; e.g., the application of the rule assumes that the environment be read as:

$$
\left\{
\begin{array}{l}
\text{C } (╪) \begin{bmatrix} \alpha\text{voc} \\ \alpha\text{cns} \end{bmatrix} \\[2ex]
\left[\begin{bmatrix} +\text{obs} \\ +\text{nas} \end{bmatrix} \right] (╪) \; [+\text{obs}]
\end{array}
\right\} ╪ \underline{\quad} \text{C}
$$

thus differing from the environment stated in rule (ii) in the insertion of the two morpheme boundaries in parentheses.

James McCawley has suggested a convention that obviates the specification of boundaries in rules unless they are necessary for the application of a rule (McCawley, 1965: 48–55). Given the two rules:

(i) $\quad [+\text{nas}] \longrightarrow \begin{bmatrix} \alpha\text{grv} \\ \beta\text{high} \end{bmatrix} \; / \; \underline{\quad} (╪) \begin{bmatrix} +\text{cns} \\ \alpha\text{grv} \\ \beta\text{high} \end{bmatrix}$

(ii) $\quad [+\text{nas}] \longrightarrow \begin{bmatrix} \alpha\text{grv} \\ \beta\text{high} \end{bmatrix} \; / \; \underline{\quad} \begin{bmatrix} +\text{cns} \\ \alpha\text{grv} \\ \beta\text{high} \end{bmatrix}$

McCawley argues that Rule (i) is more general than Rule (ii). Yet within a framework that treats boundaries in the same manner as other segments, Rule (i) will contain more symbols than (ii); consequently, greater generality does not correspond to greater simplicity.

McCawley's argument in itself is not compelling, however, since '__(r)V' is also more general than '__V', but will necessarily give a higher feature count. The type of generality involved in the '(‡)' situation is fundamentally different from that involved in the '(r)' situation. If boundaries are treated in the same manner as other segments, numerous rules will require 'boundary in parentheses' specifications, and, indeed, they usually lead to complexity in situations where the boundaries have nothing to do with the phonological constraints stated by the rule, such as in the nasal assimilation Rule (i) above.

According to McCawley's proposed convention for boundary symbols, the difference between Rules (i) and (ii) above lies in a condition imposed upon Rule (ii) which prohibits it from applying across a word boundary, whereas Rule (i) has no such constraint. McCawley further hypothesizes that boundary phenomena in all languages behave in a hierarchical manner: morpheme boundary at the lowest level, pause boundary at the highest level, and various other boundaries, such as word boundary, in-between. I propose the following feature analysis to express this hierarchy: All boundaries are at least a morpheme boundary, all pause boundaries are also word boundaries, but no lower boundaries are pause boundaries:

	⊦	‡		
morpheme	+	+	+
word	−	+	+
pause	−	−	+

The features 'morpheme', 'word', and 'pause' may be interpreted as constraints upon the domain covered by a given rule, such that a 'word-level' rule will be one that blocks application of the rule across any boundary for which the feature 'word' is marked 'plus'. This differs slightly from McCawley's approach, which does not use features, but uses the terms 'rank ‡', etc., to correspond to 'word level', etc. The difference between Rules (i) and (ii) above can be stated as a difference in level of application. Thus (i) will be a 'pause-level' rule, and the boundary in parentheses can be deleted; (ii) will be a 'morpheme-level' rule.

Chomsky and Halle have claimed that morpheme-level P rules do not occur (cf. McCawley, 1965: 54)—i.e., no rule that is restricted in application to a single morpheme will apply after some rule applying across morpheme boundaries, and this might seem reasonable in light of the fact that phonological constraints within morphemes are the concern of the morpheme-structure component. Eugene Loos (1967), however, presents evidence for several such P rules in Capanahua. Further, in light of the numerous available devices for rule formation, it is likely that any situation calling for a morpheme-level P rule could be reformulated in conformance with the above claim. Donald Becker has called my attention to the fact that the Zürich German Rule (xxxvi) in Chapter 7, which must apply after the umlaut P rule, can more directly reflect the generalization in question if we allow the rule to be 'morpheme-level'; thus:

$$\text{(iii)} \atop \text{morpheme-level:} \begin{bmatrix} +\text{syl} \\ +\text{cmp} \\ -\text{grv} \\ +\text{flt} \end{bmatrix} \longrightarrow \begin{bmatrix} -\text{cmp} \\ -\text{tns} \\ \langle -\text{flt} \rangle \end{bmatrix} / \langle \ — \ C_0 \begin{bmatrix} -\text{syl} \\ -\text{cns} \\ -\text{grv} \end{bmatrix} \rangle$$

i.e., a low, front, rounded vowel becomes nonlow and lax, and, in addition, is unrounded before [y].

The following feature table indicates the type of hierarchy commonly found in a language such as Finnish. Allowance has been made for a special boundary '&', which handles the domain of vowel harmony, not always coterminous with word boundaries.

	+	&	‡	|
morpheme	+	+	+	+
harmony	−	+	+	+
word	−	−	+	+
phrase	−	−	−	+

A harmony-level rule will automatically make the word the domain of the vowel-harmony rule, unless the word contains a '&' boundary, since both ‡ and & are '+harmony', e.g., ‡täl&laisena‡ *as this kind* (< tä+n *this* (gen.) plus the back-vowel adjective formative lais and nA 'essive'), ‡isänänsäkö‡ *as his father?* (< isä *father* + nA 'essive' + nsA 'third person possessive' + kO 'interrogative'). The primary function of the ‡ boundary in Finnish is to determine the domain of stress.

If Rules (i) and (ii) now differ only in level or rank specification, the problem of relating simplicity to generality remains to be dealt with. McCawley suggests that the highest member of the junctural hierarchy be assumed by convention in all rules that are not otherwise assigned a lower rank (i.e., it can be treated as the unmarked case). This provides the most general solution with regard to the number of parenthesized junctures it logically obviates. But, as noted above, the basic argument here has little to do with the use of parentheses. From an empirical point of view, in languages with a clearly developed word structure, pause-level rules are relatively rare and the word level appears to be the most suitable candidate for the unmarked case. Most of the P rules in the preceding sections have been assumed to be word-level rules. One exception is the English stress Rule (i) (Chapter 9) presented in the discussion of rule cycles, which is a phrase-level rule. Perhaps the unmarked level is a matter to be determined independently for each language. I suspect that it can be shown, in part, to be subject to areal influence in a manner similar to other prosodic phenomena.

By using the above feature table, a further distinction can be made between the relative economy of the phrase-level and the harmony-level constraints. If those features which are nondistinctive are deleted, making the maximum use of 'minus' features, the following system is found:

	&	‡	|
word	−	(+)	0
phrase	−	(−)	+

In this manner, any special boundary between the morpheme and the word level would give a higher feature count than the highest member of the hierarchy. This also agrees well with the feeling that junctures such as '&' are ad hoc and should count more than a phrase-level juncture.

One other advantage to the above approach to juncture systems is that no rules need be given for the deletion of the boundaries from the phonetic output of the string. From McCawley's point of view, all elements in the string that do not receive a physical phonetic value are simply not pronounced.

Regardless of the level or rank limitation on rules, a rule of any rank may require the presence of any juncture. For example, rule (ii) in

Chapter 9 is a word-level rule, but its environment contains a morpheme boundary '$+$' (cf. also Rule (xxiv) in Chapter 7.)

The above feature representation offers certain advantages in considering the rules for boundary insertion. In one approach to boundary insertion, a low-level transformational rule such as (iv) will insert a word boundary between all lexical items in the utterance.

(iv)

$$SD: \quad X^\frown Y^\frown Z \text{ where Y is a lexical category}$$
$$1 \quad 2 \quad 3$$

$$SC: \quad 1 \;^\frown \; + \;^\frown \; 2 \;^\frown \; + \;^\frown \; 3$$

Later rules will insert affixes from syntactic and lexical features contained within the base forms obtained from the lexicon; e.g., in Russian the following rule can be used to insert the /a/ ending for the masculine-neuter genetive singular of nouns:

(v)

$$SD: \quad N$$
$$[-\text{fem}, +\text{sg}, +\text{gen}]$$
$$1$$

$$SC: \quad 1 \longrightarrow 1^\frown a$$

thus giving a string $+^\frown N^\frown a^\frown +$. The desirability of such a rule becomes apparent when we consider the fact that the features in the structural description stem from diverse sources: (a) The gender of the noun must be listed in the lexicon; (b) Its number is provided by the base rules; and (c) The case of nouns is determined by transformational rules—as a result of verb or preposition government, or in conjunction with certain constructions. Finally, a very general convention will insert morpheme boundaries between all elements in the string; e.g.,

(vi)

$$SD: \quad X^\frown Y$$
$$1 \quad 2$$

$$SC: \quad 1^\frown +^\frown 2$$

The Convention (vi) must either exclude word boundaries from its structural description or provide that any sequence of two boundaries drop that boundary which is lower in the hierarchy. Thus the convention could be adopted that when two boundaries occur in sequence, if either boundary is marked 'plus' for any given feature for which the other is

...arked 'minus', the boundary with the 'minus' feature is deleted, thus:

(vii)   SD: $\begin{bmatrix} +\text{boundary} \\ +F_i \end{bmatrix}$, $\begin{bmatrix} +\text{boundary} \\ -F_i \end{bmatrix}$
                        1   2

(where no sequential order is imposed
upon 1, 2)

SC: 2 ⟶ null

...lsewhere, either boundary is deleted.

Special boundaries, such as the above harmony juncture in Finnish, ...ill no doubt be produced on the basis of morpheme features belonging ...o certain morphemes in the sentence. A rule such as the following may ...e desirable:

(viii) $+$ ⟶ [+harmony] / _____ [+harmony]

...e., a morpheme boundary acquires the feature [+harmony] (> &) ...efore a morpheme containing that feature.

For any rules cited in above sections that make specific reference to ...he word boundary '$+$' (e.g., Rule (xx) in Chapter 7), it should be clear ...hat any higher-level boundary would also satisfy the structural descrip-...ion; thus, for a word in phrase-final position, the Latin stress rule will ...ave to count vowel morae from the final phrase boundary instead of ...rom a word boundary (assuming that the sequence '$+^-|$' is not allowed). ...o handle this situation McCawley (1966: 8) sets up five ranked boun-...laries for Finnish, ranging from morpheme boundary at the top to ...hrase boundary at the bottom, and rules that 'an occurrence of any ...f these boundaries also counts as an occurrence of any "lower" boun-...lary.' Thus in the above Latin example, a '$+$' specified in the rule would ...lso count as a '|' boundary. In terms of the above feature representation ...f the junctures, McCawley's convention can be reformulated as follows:

| | indicates any boundary which |
the rule symbol	has the feature(s)
$+$	+morpheme
&	+harmony (+morpheme)
$\ddagger$	+word (+harmony, +morpheme)
		+phrase (+word, +harmony, +morpheme)

Given the above feature representation, boundary references in th structural description of a rule receive the same interpretation as seg mental references—i.e., a condition which must be met if the rule is t apply; for example, a '$+$' indicates any boundary that has the featur '$+$word' rather than '$\ddagger$ and only $+$'. McCawley's special conventio would, then, no longer be necessary.

The above boundary-feature approach also provides a reasonabl way of assigning a value to junctures within the simplicity metric. Eac reference to a boundary symbol in a rule receives a value of '1' for ever 'plus' feature which it assumes; thus a reference to a '$+$' boundary, wit a count of '1' plus feature is more general than a reference to a '$\ddagger$ boundary (with a count of '4' plus features).

The use of boundary features in rules may be desirable, as in th *n*-deletion rule of Alsatian German (cf. Becker, 1967). (Here the bound ary is indicated by a '$+$morpheme boundary' segment.)

(ix)

$$[+\text{nas}] \longrightarrow \text{null} \ / \ \begin{bmatrix} +\text{syl} \\ +\text{grv} \\ -\text{flt} \end{bmatrix} - \begin{bmatrix} +\text{morpheme boundary} \\ \langle -\text{phrase boundary}\rangle_a \end{bmatrix} \langle C \rangle_b$$

Condition: If a, then b.

i.e., [n] is lost after a grave, unrounded vowel before any boundary plu a consonant, or in phrase-final position (where the boundary i '$+$phrase'). The environment can also be expressed as:

$$\begin{bmatrix} +\text{syl} \\ +\text{grv} \\ -\text{flt} \end{bmatrix} - \begin{Bmatrix} | \\ +C \end{Bmatrix}$$

but it does not reflect the generalization as directly as the above featur environment.

B. The syllable. Little has been said concerning the role of syllable in generative phonology. Rather than operate with the syllable as unit of some kind, even in rules in which the syllable appears to be relevant category, linguists have tended to spell out the segmental en vironment necessary for the satisfactory operation of the rule; e.g Finnish has a rule such as the following:

$$(\text{x}) \quad \begin{bmatrix} +\text{syl} \\ +\text{low} \\ -\text{grv} \end{bmatrix} \longrightarrow \begin{bmatrix} -\text{low} \\ +\text{flt} \end{bmatrix} \ / \ \ddagger \ C_0 V_1 C_1 VCk\_ i \ +$$

.e., a stem-final [ä] in the third syllable after [k] becomes [ö] before
he morpheme -i- (e.g., [nypykkä┤i┤nä] > [nypykköinä] *as tips*). The
·ule achieves the desired result, but the objection can be raised here that
he relevant generalization is lost in the sequence of C's and V's required
₀o indicate a domain of two syllables. In an attempt to improve upon
he earlier approach to syllable representation, McCawley proposes the
ıse of a symbol 'S' (syllable) in his description of Japanese (1965: 55–60).
He presents the following two rules with 'S' (the first is hypothetical;
₌he second is from the Nagasaki dialect (p. 210)):

$$(\text{xi}) \qquad \text{S} \longrightarrow [3 \text{ stress}] \ / \ \_\text{S} \quad \underset{1 \text{ stress}}{\text{S}}$$

.e., the second syllable before a primary-stressed syllable receives
·3 stress'.

$$(\text{xii}) \quad \text{S} \longrightarrow [+\text{high pitch}] \ / \ \underset{+\text{falling}}{\ddagger(\text{S})} \ \_ \ \text{S}\ldots)$$

..e., for words marked '+falling', those with three or more syllables
·eceive high pitch on the second syllable; those with two syllables, on
the first syllable.

The above use of 'S' assumes that 'a feature belonging to the ...
syllable can be referred to as if it belonged to one of the segments of
that ... syllable' (p. 60). If certain prosodic features such as tone, accent,
₀r stress are understood by convention to be syllable-level features, then
ı rule such as (xiii) 'will mean "put accent on the *syllable* which contains
the third from last mora"' (60).

$$(\text{xiii}) \qquad \text{V} \longrightarrow [+\text{acc}] \ / \ \_(\text{C})\text{V}(\text{C})\text{V}\ddagger$$

The element 'S' will require rules that provide an interpretation of
₌ach utterance as a sequence of syllables. At the level of systematic
phonemics, Finnish syllable boundaries ('.') can be inserted by Rule
ₓxiv).

$$(\text{xiv}) \qquad \text{null} \longrightarrow . \ / \ \left\{ \begin{array}{c} \_\text{CV} \\ \text{V}' \_ \left[\begin{array}{c} +\text{syl} \\ -\text{high} \end{array} \right]'' \end{array} \right\}$$

Condition: V' does not equal V''.

Rule (x) can now be restated in a manner that directly reflects the underlying generalization:

$$\text{(xv)} \quad \begin{bmatrix} +\text{syl} \\ +\text{low} \\ -\text{grv} \end{bmatrix} \longrightarrow \begin{bmatrix} -\text{low} \\ +\text{flt} \end{bmatrix} \; / \; \ddagger S_2^2 \, k\underline{\quad}\dagger i\dagger$$

The loss of consonants in later Finnish rules will call for further shifting or removal of certain syllable boundaries at a low-level phonetic stage, but for the most part these changes will be minor: e.g., [raa.kan] > [ra : .an], but [ya.kan] > [ya:n], [ma.kuis.sa] > [ma.uis.sa] > [mauis.sa].

Syllable boundaries will stand apart from the above system of levels for handling syntactically and morphologically determined boundary devices. On the other hand, the convention for omitting from rules all boundaries that are not required for the application of the rules will also apply here. A given phonological string may have simultaneous morpheme and syllable boundaries, e.g., Finnish [‡.ta.lo†.ta‡], [‡.raa.ka†s.sa‡].

C. Morpheme features. In addition to its phonological feature matrix, a morpheme may also contain morpheme features. In a manner similar to the syllable features discussed above, any feature pertaining to a morpheme as a whole can also be considered as occurring in any segment of the morpheme.

Morpheme features treat a wide variety of situations that cannot satisfactorily be described in purely phonological terms. Often, certain morphemes do not undergo rules that otherwise appear to be general phonological processes of the language in question. For instance, for Finnish bases with an -hk- cluster, it is not possible to predict which ones will undergo the consonant gradation rule (k > null), e.g., /nahka†n/ > [nahan] *skin* (gen.), /pahka†n/ > [pahkan] *lump* (gen.). In this situation, the morpheme *pahka* will be assigned a *rule feature* that blocks application of the gradation rule, say, [− Rule P26]. Or, on the other hand, certain morphemes are subject to special rules that do not affect most other morphemes. In colloquial Finnish final [i] is dropped after [s], but only for a list of ten or so morphemes, e.g., [viisi] > [viis] *five*, but [liesi] *hearth* (cf. Harms, 1964: 22–23). These ten morphemes would be assigned a special feature which will be necessary for the application of the rule in question, say, [+ Rule P6].

Rules that are general for morphemes in the language are called *major rules*; rules that apply only to special morphemes are called *minor rules* (cf. Lakoff, 1965). All morphemes are by convention considered to be 'plus' for any major rule and 'minus' for any minor rule—except those morphemes which possess specially assigned rule features to the contrary, as in the above Finnish examples. Thus the Finnish rule for [i] deletion will be listed as a minor rule, and only those few morphemes which are marked 'plus' for that rule can undergo the change, provided that they otherwise satisfy the structural description of the rule.

Consider also the situation where a major rule applies to certain morphemes that do not otherwise satisfy the structural description of the rule. In Finnish, intervocalic [t] is normally dropped after an un-stressed (i.e., noninitial syllable) vowel, but retained elsewhere; thus, /talo┼ta/ > [taloa], but /si┼ta/ > [sitä]. The colloquial first and second pronoun forms, which are monosyllabic, also undergo the rule, e.g., [mu┼ta] > [mua]. Here the morphemes /mu/ *I* and /su/ *you* will be assigned a feature that indicates that they satisfy the environment re-quired for the *t*-deletion rule regardless of their segmental qualification; e.g., [+SD of P15]. This solution is very close to certain traditional descriptions of Finnish in which /mu/ and /su/ are described as 'un-stressed' pronouns—but the 'stress' in question here could only be mor-phological and has nothing to do with the phonetic stress of the forms.

Frequently, a limited class of morphemes, generally lexical forms, will be characterized by numerous shared major and minor rule con-straints. Foreign and so-called descriptive morphemes commonly par-ticipate in such morpheme classes. In Komi, normal, native words do not permit initial consonant clusters. In words of recent foreign origin, mostly Russian, and in certain words describing sounds and sudden actions, initial clusters are permitted. The clusters in the two types of words, however, do not follow the same constraints. Two special sets of MS rules will be necessary to handle these two classes of forms; e.g., only descriptive words will be subject to the following rule:

(xvi) $[+\text{descriptive}] \longrightarrow \begin{bmatrix} +\text{voc} \\ -\text{cns} \end{bmatrix} / \text{┼CC\_\_}$

i.e., no initial three-consonant clusters are allowed; e.g., /zvirkńit/ *leap up* (cf. however, the Russian loan /strəit/ *build*).

Morphemes of this sort will be specified '+foreign', '+descriptive', etc. The rules in question may also be specified for these features, with the convention that the rules apply only to morphemes with the corresponding feature. McCawley uses morpheme features as constraints in the environments of rules (1965; cf. Rule (viii) in Chapter 8). Or perhaps a type of MS rule for morpheme features could add the appropriate rule features to the morphemes in question, e.g.,

$$
\text{(xvii)} \qquad [+\text{foreign}] \longrightarrow
\begin{bmatrix}
-\text{rules MS 1–4} \\
+\text{rules MS 18–24} \\
-\text{rules P 13, 26} \\
+\text{rule P 10} \\
+\text{SD of rule P3}
\end{bmatrix}
$$

Certain MS rules for morpheme features will be needed regardless of the manner in which classes such as [+foreign] are interpreted. In Finnish, proper nouns with a single noninitial stop are not subject to consonant gradation, e.g., /sirpa+n/ > [sirpan] *Sirpa's*, but /orpo+n/ > [orvon] *the orphan's*. Proper nouns with a geminate stop, however, undergo the general rule, e.g., /hilppa+n/ > [hilpan] *Hilppa's*. The following rule adds a minus rule feature to the *Sirpa*-type proper nouns:

$$
\text{(xviii)} \quad
\begin{bmatrix}
+\text{N} \\
+\text{proper} \\
+\text{obs} \\
-\text{cnt}
\end{bmatrix}
\longrightarrow [-\text{Rule P26}] \ / \ [-\text{obs}] \ \underline{\hspace{2em}} \ \text{V}
$$

In the same manner as Rule (xiii) (for syllable features), Rule (xviii) adds the minus rule feature for the entire morpheme whose segments satisfy the structural description.

From the above discussion it may be seen that morpheme features lead to phonological generality in several ways. First, forms that deviate from the generally recognized patterns of a language can be treated as special subsystems, exhibiting regularities of their own. This corresponds well with the speaker's ability to spot words of foreign origin on a purely phonological basis, and explains why the creation of new descriptive forms tends to be subject to special constraints. The taxonomic tendency to collapse all phonetic phenomena to a single plane of description often led to phonemic contrasts and phonotactic statements that were skewed by the inclusion of loanwords and other words of special status, thus obscuring generalizations in all subsystems.

Secondly, processes that are phonological are sharply set off from those which are lexically or grammatically determined. (Compare, for instance, the use of capital-letter morphophonemes in Harms, 1964, which tends to obscure the difference between the various types of conditioning in phonological rules.)

Thirdly, boundary markers (other than morpheme boundary) can be reserved for processes that involve domains of application that are greater than a single morpheme. (Compare Harms, 1966b, where a special boundary '=' is set up solely to prevent the general rule which specifies the vowels of all suffixes as nongrave from applying to a small number of derivational morphemes. These exceptional morphemes should more properly be handled by a rule feature.)

EXERCISES

1. Characterize the following dialect differences:
   (a) For certain Estonian speakers, a syllabification contrast exists between a sequence of [vətta] *take!* plus [nemat] *them* and [vəttan] *I take* plus [emat] *mothers*: [vət.ta.ne.mat] versus [vət.tan.e.mat]; for other speakers, however, both sequences are [vət.ta.ne.mat].
   (b) In Standard Finnish, underlying final /k/ is assimilated to any following consonant except [h y] (the only glides) within the same phrase: [tulek+pas/ > [tuleppas]   *do   come!*,   /tulek+nopetasti/ > [tulen‡ nopeasti] *come quickly!*, /tulek‡tänäsen/ > [tulet‡tänään] *come today!*. In certain other Finnish dialects, this assimilation is limited to following affixes within the same word: /tulek+pas/ > [tuleppas] *do come!*, /satek+ta/ > [saitta] *rain* (part.) (cf. Itkonen, 1964: 154).

2. Nez Perce has the five vowels /u e i a o/ (both long and short), but in any given word the vowel sets [u e i] and [o a i] are mutually exclusive, e.g.,

naʔtó : t	*my father*
tó : taʔ	*father!*
neʔméx	*my paternal uncle*
méqeʔ	*paternal uncle!* (q > x in final position)
tísqeʔ	*skunk*
tísqaʔlaykin	*near a skunk*
wé : yik	*go across* (stem)
wé : yikse	*(I) am going across*
watwá : yiksa	*(I) am wading across.*

We are told that 'the sequence in which only the set ... (i̱ e̱ u̱) or the set ... (i̱ a̱ o̱) occurs is not always coterminous with the morphological word, e.g. ... /‡cú : łeʼmayn‡/ *for the bull.*' (Aoki, 1966: 760).

Establish the underlying representations of the above words and write the rule that determines vowel harmony. What 'level' is the rule?

3. Cairo Arabic verb roots must be described as having emphatic and non-emphatic underlying consonants. It has been noted that 'the distribution of [phonetic] emphasis always coincides with syllable boundaries; a syllable has all or none of its sounds emphatic' (Lehn and Abboud, 1965: 271). Note the following examples (emphatic sounds are underlined):

1.	ṭawi : l	*long*
2.	ṭawi : la	*long* (fem.)
3.	ṭuwa : l	*long* (pl.)
4.	gidi : d	*new*
5.	guda : d	*new* (pl.)
6.	laṭi : f	*pleasant*
7.	mišlaṭi : f	*unpleasant*
8.	laṭi : fa	*pleasant* (fem.)
9.	ša : tir	*clever*
10.	šaṭra	*clever* (fem.)
11.	ḥarra : n	*hot*
12.	ḥarra : na	*hot* (fem.)
13.	xarag	*he went out*
14.	xaragit	*she went out*
15.	xarakt	*you* (masc.) *went out*
16.	yuxrug	*he goes out*
17.	biyuxrug	*he is going out*
18.	daxal	*he entered*
19.	daxalit	*she entered*
20.	daxalt	*you* (masc.) *entered*
21.	yudxul	*he enters*
22.	di šanṭiṭ sitt	*this is a lady's purse*
23.	di šanṭiṭ⌢issitt	*this is the lady's purse* (is- < il- 'def.')
24.	dira : sa	*study*

(a) Indicate the underlying emphatic consonants in the above words (assuming the MS rules to have applied). Why has underlying emphasis been assigned to the consonants?

(b) Since uvular consonants /q x γ/, pharyngeals /ħ ʕ/, and rounded vowels occur both as emphatic and nonemphatic /cf. [ħuma : r] *donkey*, [ħuku : ma] *government*), what feature can be used to account for emphasis? In articulatory terms, 'the tongue is slightly retracted, laterally spread, and the back is raised .... At the same time, the lips are held neutral (not spread as for the plain sounds) or slightly protruded or rounded. The articulatory features plus increased tenseness of the throat muscles combine to give the emphatics a "hollow sound" '

(Lehn and Abboud, 1965: 271). Is it desirable to have a given feature function independently on the segmental and syllable levels?

(c) State the rule that determines phonetic emphasis.

(d) Is it desirable to specify the rule as 'syllable level'?

4. Huichol stress phenomena have been described in terms of syllabic pitch and a syllable-sequence domain labeled 'foot' (=phonological phrase). The following statements govern stress occurrence (Grimes, 1959: 225):

1. 'If the pitch in a foot drops, the last syllable with the higher pitch is stressed: há³ke² .... Where? (*incredulously*) ....'

2. 'If the pitch rises from pitch 1, and if the first syllable is long and succeeding syllables are short, the first syllable is stressed: téʌ¹te¹ri² + [yáa³ri¹] *type of people* ....'

3. 'If the pitch rises from pitch 1, the first syllable of higher pitch is stressed: tee¹pʌʌ³ *flea* ....'

4. 'If the pitch is level, or if it rises from pitch 2, and if the first syllable, begins with /ʔ/, is short, and is followed by a long syllable, the second syllable is stressed: ʔu³tái³ *giant woodpecker* ....'

5. 'The first syllable is stressed: ... tá³ciu³ *rabbit* ....'

'1' is the lowest pitch, '4' the highest. A 'short syllable' contains only a single vowel peak and does not end in a consonant; a 'long syllable' ends in a consonant or has a two-vowel peak. Note that the above conditions are ordered in the sense that an earlier rule precedes and excludes any later rules.

Formulate appropriate feature rules to account for the above phenomena; also, present a rule to specify the syllable feature 'long'.

5. In one Mixtec dialect, tone phenomena are described in terms of underlying tone couplets which occur on given morphemes. In certain syntactic constructions, such as noun plus modifier, noun compounds, locative plus noun and verb plus noun modifier, the following changes in underlying tone are observed (where '3' is the highest tone, '1' the lowest):

underlying tone	second couplet becomes	underlying tone	second couplet becomes
3-1 + 3-3	1-3	3-3 + 1-1	3-1
2-1 + 3-3	1-3	2-3 + 1-1	3-1
1-1 + 3-3	1-3	1-3 + 1-1	3-1
1-1 + 2-3	1-3	2-2 + 1-1	3-1
1-1 + 2-2	1-3	1-1 + 1-1	3-1
3-3 + 2-3	3-3	3-3 + 1-3	₃⌢1-3
2-3 + 2-3	3-3	2-3 + 1-3	₃⌢1-3
1-3 + 2-3	3-3	2-2 + 1-3	₃⌢1-3
3-2 + 2-3	3-3	2-1 + 1-3	₃⌢1-3

2-2 + 2-3	3-3	1-1 + 1-3	$_3\frown$1-3
3-3 + 2-2	3-2	2-3 + 1-2	$_3\frown$1-2
2-3 + 2-2	3-3	2-2 + 1-2	$_3\frown$1-2
1-3 + 2-2	3-3	1-2 + 1-2	$_3\frown$1-2
2-2 + 2-2	3-3	1-1 + 1-2	$_3\frown$1-2
3-3 + 2-1	3-1		
2-3 + 2-1	3-1		
1-3 + 2-1	3-1		
2-2 + 2-1	3-1		
1-1 + 2-1	3-1		

EXAMPLES: ka³ži¹ *street* + ka³ni³ *long* > ka³ži¹‡ka¹ni³ *long street*,
ʔi²či² *road* + ža¹ta¹ *back* > ʔi²či²‡ža³ta¹ *behind*
ha¹a¹ *that thing* + ba¹ʔa² *good* > ha¹a¹‡ba³¹ʔa² *the good*.
If one of the special constructions consists of three tone couplets, then
normally only the last couplet is affected:
2-2 + 2-1 + 1-2 > 2-2 + 2-1 + $_3\frown$1-2.
[$_3\frown$1] or [31] are falling tones (from [3] to [1]). The dialect also has a [13]
rising tone.
When a verb is syntactically 'continuative' (no affix), 'deliberative'
(na³−), or 'causative' (s−), the following changes occur:

underlying tone	modified tone
2-3	3-3
2-2	3-2
2-1	3-1
1-3	$_3\frown$1-3
1-2	$_3\frown$1-2
1-1	3-1

Construct rules to account for the various alternations. Use only binary
features such as 'high', low', etc., in your rules (keeping desirable natural
classes in mind). The verb may be assumed to contain such features as
'+causative', '+continuative', in addition to the corresponding affixes.
Consider the use of such a feature as [+SD: ab__], which means that the
morpheme in question behaves as though it occurred in the environment
'ab__', regardless of its actual environment. (Based on Mak, 1958.)

6. Formulate rules to account for the various phenomena described:

(a) In Ticuna, 'the vowels, at their respective points of articulation, all
have voiceless allophonic counterparts which occur word final in words
of more than three syllables ...' (Anderson, 1959: 78).

(b) In Bravanese Swahili, phrase stress occurs on the penult, but in certain constructions final stress is regular: (a) with the first and second person forms of the present and preterite tenses, (b) with the past conditional, and (c) with the negative imperative (among others). (Based on Goodman, 1967.)

EXAMPLES:

ye naxsó : ma	*he is reading*
we naxso : má	*you* (sing.) *are reading*
we some : ré	*you* (sing.) *read* (past)
ye somé : re	*he read*
só : ma	*read*!
siso : mé	*don't read*!

(c) In Finnish, morpheme-final [a ä] is replaced by [e] in:

1. Two-syllable noun and adjective stems before the comparative suffix /mpä/, except for /kiva/ *cute*:

halpa+mpä > halvempi *cheaper*
rusketa+mpä > ruskeampi *browner*
kiva+mpä > kivampi *cuter*

2. Any verb stems before the impersonal suffix [ttä]: anta+ttä+h+sen > annetaan *one gives* (other [ttä] suffixes do not cause this change);
3. The infinitive [tä] before the inessive [ssä] and instructive [n] cases:

anta+tä+ssä > antaessa *in giving*
tul+tä+n > tullen *coming*

(d) Manchurian has the following stem pairs:

1.	ama	*father*
	eme	*mother*
2.	xaxa	*man*
	xexe	*woman*
3.	amxa	*father-in-law*
	emxe	*mother-in-law*
4.	nača	*older brother-in-law*
	neče	*brother-in-law's wife*
5.	arsalan	*lion*
	erseleń	*lioness*
6.	amila	*male*
	emile	*female*
7.	gangań	*strong*
	gengeń	*weak*

General phonological rules for vowel harmony cannot be given for Manchurian. (Based on Paškov, 1963.)

(e) In addition to the rules for Yoruba vowel contraction presented in Exercise 1 of Chapter 9, the following ordered statements must also be made (Bamgboṣe, 1965: 26–27):

1. 'The initial low tone syllable of a nominal (other than ì) is ... retained': kɔ́ ɛ̀kɔ́ > kɛ́kɔ́ *learn a lesson*..
2. 'The initial vowel of a nominal whose first two syllables consist of two identical vowels is ... retained': ra oògùn > roògùn *buy medicine.*
3. 'The vowel [a] of a verb having a high tone is ..., retained, except in the case of [bá] and [wá] where this vowel is elided': já ewé > jáwé *pluck the leaves*, wá ɛja > wɛ́ja *look for fish.*
4. 'The vowel [a] of a verb which has a midtone when followed by a complement is ... retained ...': ka owó > kawó *count the money.*
5. Elsewhere the vowel of the verb is lost: kó ewé > kéwé *gather the leaves.*

In the above contractions, a high plus a low or midtone results in a high tone.

7. Polish masculine and neuter (as opposed to feminine) noun stems show the following two forms of the prepositional singular case suffix. (Neuter nouns take the endings [o] or [e] in the nominative.) Give the rule(s) for the prepositional case insertion.

	nom.	prep.
oven	ṕec	ṕecu
guest	gośč	gośču
bear	ńeʒ́več	neʒ́veʒu
plate	tal'eš	tal'ežu
basket	koš	košu
sea	može	možu
goal	cel'	cel'u
field	pol'e	pol'u
uncle	vuy	vuyu
horse	koń	końu
sentence	zdańe	zdańu
sky	ńebo	ńeb'e
brother	brat	brače
holiday	šv́ēto	šv́ēče
government	žõt	žõʒe
flock	stado	staʒe
nose	nos	noše
iron	želazo	želaže

lake	yežoro	yežože
glass	šklo	škl′e
general	general	general′e
butter	maslo	mašl′e
tone	ton	tońe
window	okno	okńe

8. In Classical Greek, certain aspects of verb reduplication may be described as follows (ignoring certain exceptions):

1. In the perfect and future perfect:

(a) A verb beginning with a single consonant other than /r/, or with a stop plus liquid, prefixes the initial consonant plus [e]:

lūō	I release
leluka	I have released
pʰainō	I show
pepʰasmai	I have appeared
grapʰō	I write
gegrapʰa	I have written
kʰainō	I gape
kekʰēna	I have gaped
tinō	I pay
tetīka	I have paid

(b) Certain verbs have an [ei] prefix in the perfect instead of reduplication:

lakʰ- : eilēkʰa	I have obtained by lot
re- : eirēka	I have said

(c) Verbs beginning with other consonant clusters or with /r/ prefix an [e]:

stellō	I send
estalka	I have sent

2. For verbs with consonant reduplication in the perfect, the pluperfect prefixes an [e] to the reduplication:

eielukē   *I had released*

3. A few verbs reduplicate the present by prefixing the initial consonant plus [i]:

gno- : gignōskō	I know
tʰē- : titʰēmi	I stand

Note further the following stem-consonant alternations:

(a) trik^hos   *hair* (gen.)
    t^hriks   *hair* (nom.)
(b) amp^hi   *about*
    ek^hō   *I have*
    ampek^hō   *I wrap about*
(c) trek^hō   *I run*
    t^hreksomai   *I shall run*

Write rules for the above verb prefixation and reduplication phenomena, ignoring stem and suffix changes other than the aspiration alternations. Indicate those features which must be listed in the lexicon and those features which have been syntactically determined. (Based on Goodwin, 1892.)

Selected Bibliography

Bach, Emmon, 1964. *An Introduction to Transformational Grammars*. New York.

———, 1966. "Two Proposals Concerning the Simplicity Metric in Phonology". Paper read before the Linguistic Society of America. New York.

———, 1967. "Some Notes on Igbo Phonology". Dittoed, Austin.

Becker, Donald A., 1967. "Generative Phonology and Dialect Study: An Investigation of Three Modern German Dialects". Unpublished dissertation, University of Texas at Austin.

Bloch, Bernard, and George L. Trager, 1942. *Outline of Linguistic Analysis*. Baltimore.

Browne, E. W., and James D. McCawley, 1965. "Srpskohrvatski akcenat". *Zbornik za filologiju i lingvistiku*, **8**: pp. 147–51.

Carrell, Patricia L. G., 1966. "A Transformational Grammar of Igbo". Unpublished dissertation, University of Texas at Austin.

Cherry, E. Colin, Morris Halle, and Roman Jakobson, 1953. "Toward the Logical Description of Languages in Their Phonemic Aspect", in *Language* **29**: pp. 34–46.

Chomsky, Noam, 1964. "Current Issues in Linguistic Theory". In Fodor and Katz: pp. 50–118.

———, 1965. *Aspects of the Theory of Syntax*. Cambridge, Mass.

Chomsky, Noam, and Morris Halle, 1965. "Some Controversial Questions in Phonological Theory", in *Journal of Linguistics* **1**: pp. 97–138.

———, to appear. *The Sound Pattern of English*. New York.

Chomsky, Noam, and George A. Miller, 1963. "Introduction to the Formal Analysis of Natural Languages", in *Handbook of Mathematical Psychology*: **II**, pp. 269–321. Edited by R. Duncan Luce, Robert R. Bush, and Eugene Galanter. New York and London.

Fodor, Jerry A., and Jerrold J. Katz, eds., 1964. *The Structure of Language.* Englewood Cliffs, N. J.

Halle, Morris, 1959. *The Sound Pattern of Russian.* The Hague.

———, 1961. "Note on Cyclically Ordered Rules in the Russian Conjugation", in *Quarterly Progress Report No. 63*, M.I.T. Research Laboratory of Electronics, pp. 149–55. Cambridge, Mass.

———, 1962a. "A Descriptive Convention for Treating Assimilation and Dissimilation". In *Quarterly Progress Report No. 66*, M.I.T. Research Laboratory of Electronics, pp. 295–96. Cambridge, Mass.

———, 1962b. "Phonology in Generative Grammar", in *Word*, **18**, pp. 54–72. Reprinted in Fodor and Katz, 1964: pp. 334–52.

———, 1963. "O pravilax russkogo sprjaženija", in *American Contributions to the Fifth International Congress of Slavists*, I (identical with *Slavistic Printings and Reprintings*, **XLVI**), pp. 113–32. The Hague.

———, 1964. "On the Bases of Phonology", in Fodor and Katz, 1964: pp. 324–33.

———, 1966. "Variables as Coefficients of Features". Paper read at the University of Texas Symposium on Phonology at Austin.

Harms, Robert T, 1964. *Finnish Structural Sketch* (identical with *Indiana University Publications Uralic and Altaic Series*, **42**). Bloomington, Indiana, and The Hague.

———, 1966a. "Stress, Voice, and Length in Southern Paiute". *IJAL*, **32**: pp. 228–35.

———, 1966b. "The Measurement of Phonological Economy", in *Language*, **42**: pp. 602–11.

———, 1967. "Split, Shift and Merger in the Permic Vowels". In *Ural-Altaische Jahrbücher*, **39**: pp. 163–98.

Harris, Zellig S., 1951. *Methods in Structural Linguistics.* Chicago.

Hockett, Charles F., 1955. *A Manual of Phonology. Indiana University Publications in Anthropology and Linguistics*, Memoir 11 (identical with *IJAL*, **21**, No. 4, Part 1). Baltimore.

Hoijer, Harry, 1946. "Tonkawa", in *Linguistic Structures of Native America* (identical with *Viking Fund Publications in Anthropology*, No. 6): pp. 289–311. Edited by Cornelius Osgood. New York.

Jakobson, Roman, 1957. "Mufaxxama—the 'Emphatic' Phonemes in Arabic", in *Studies Presented to Joshua Whatmough* pp. 105–15. Edited by Ernest Pulgram. The Hague. (Also in *Roman Jakobson: Selected Writings* (1962), I: pp. 510–22. The Hague.)

Jakobson, Roman, and Morris Halle, 1956. *Fundamentals of Language* (identical with *Janua Linguarum*, I). The Hague.

Jakobson, Roman, C. G. M. Fant, and Morris Halle, 1951. *Preliminaries to Speech Analysis.* Cambridge, Mass.

Keyser, Jay, 1963. "The Pronunciation of English in the Atlantic States", in *Language*, **39**: pp. 303–16. Review of Hans Kurath and Raven I. McDavid, Jr.

King, Robert D., 1966. "Root vs. Suffix Accent in the Germanic Present". Paper read before the Linguistic Society of America. New York.

Kiparsky, Paul, 1966. "Über den deutschen Akzent", in *Studia Grammatica*, **7**: pp. 69–98.

──────, 1967a. "On the History of Greek Accentuation". To appear in *Langages*.

──────, 1967b. "Linguistic Universals and Linguistic Change". Paper read at The University of Texas. To appear in *Universals in Linguistic Theory*. Edited by Emmon Bach and Robert T. Harms.

Ladefoged, Peter, 1964. *A Phonetic Study of West African Languages* (identical with *West African Language Monograph*, **I**). Cambridge, England.

Lakoff, George, 1965. *On the Nature of Syntactic Irregularity* (identical with *The Computation Laboratory of Harvard University Mathematical Linguistics and Automatic Translation Report No. NSF-16*). Cambridge, Mass.

Lightner, Theodore, M., 1963a. "A Note on the Formulation of Phonological Rules", in *Quarterly Progress Report No. 68*, M.I.T. Research Laboratory of Electronics: pp. 187–89. Cambridge, Mass.

──────, 1963b. "Remarks on the Morphophonemic Component of Russian", in *Quarterly Progress Report No. 69*, M.I.T. Research Laboratory of Electronics: pp. 193–99. Cambridge, Mass.

──────, 1965a. "Segmental Phonology of Modern Standard Russian". Unpublished dissertation, M.I.T., Cambridge, Mass.

──────, 1965b. "O cikličeskix pravilax v russkom sprjaženii", in *Voprosy jazykoznanija*, **15**: pp. 45–54.

Loos, Eugene E., 1967. "The Phonology of Capanahua and Its Grammatical Basis". Unpublished dissertation, University of Texas at Austin.

McCawley, James D., 1963. "Stress and Pitch in the Serbo-Croatian Verb", in *Quarterly Progress Report No. 70*, M.I.T. Research Laboratory of Electronics: pp. 282–90. Cambridge, Mass.

──────, 1964. "The Morphophonemics of the Finnish Noun". Dittoed, M.I.T. Cambridge, Mass.

──────, 1965. "The Accentual System of Standard Japanese". Unpublished dissertation, M.I.T. Cambridge, Mass.

──────, 1966. "Further Revisions of Finnish Rules". Dittoed, Chicago.

──────, 1967. "The Role of a Phonological Feature System in a Theory of Language". To appear in *Langages*.

Nida, Eugene A., 1949. *Morphology: The Descriptive Analysis of Words*, 2nd ed. Ann Arbor, Mich.

O'Neil, Wayne A., 1964. "Faroese Vowel Morphophonemics", in *Language* **40**: pp. 366–71.

Pike, Kenneth L., 1943. *Phonetics*. Ann Arbor, Mich.

Postal, Paul M., 1965. "On the Mentalistic Character of So-Called 'Sound Change' ". Dittoed. To appear as Part II of *Two Studies in the Theory of Phonology*.

Rohrer, Christian, 1967. "Die Behandlung der französischen Nasalvokale in der generativen Phonologie". To appear in *Probleme der strukturellen Grammatik und Semantik*. Edited by Rudolf Růžička. Leipzig.

Ross, John R., 1966. "Ablaut in German Strong Verbs". Dittoed. To appear in *Studia Grammatica*.

Sapir, Edward, 1925. "Sound Patterns in Language", in *Language*, 1: pp. 37–51. Reprinted in *Readings in Linguistics* (1957): pp. 19–25. Edited by Martin Joos. Washington.

————, 1951. "The Psychological Reality of Phonemes", in *Selected Writings of Edward Sapir in Language, Culture and Personality*: pp. 46–60. Edited by David G. Mandelbaum. Berkeley and Los Angeles.

Saporta, Sol., 1965. "Ordered Rules, Dialect Differences, and Historical Processes", in *Language*, **41**: pp. 218–24.

Sledd, James H., 1966. "Breaking, Umlaut, and the Southern Drawl", in *Language*, **42**: pp. 18–41.

Stockwell, Robert P., 1966. "Problems in the Interpretation of the Great English Vowel Shift". Dittoed. Los Angeles.

Vasiliu, Emanuel, 1966. "Transformational vs. Biunique Phonemic Typology (Towards a Classification of Dacorumanian Dialects)". Paper read at the Internationale Phonologie-Tagung, Vienna.

Wang, William S-Y., 1967. "Phonological Features of Tone", in *IJAL*, 33: pp. 93–105.

Wilson, Robert D., 1966. "A Criticism of Distinctive Features", in *Journal of Linguistics* 2: pp. 195–206.

References to Exercises

Anderson, Lambert, 1959. "Ticuna Vowels: With Special Regard to the System of Five Tonemes". *Publicações do Museo Nacional, Série Lingüistica Expecial*, **1**: pp. 76–119.

Aoki, Haruo, 1966. "Nez Perce Vowel Harmony and Proto-Sahaptian Vowels", in *Language*, **42**: pp. 759–67.

Avenesov, R. I., 1949. *Očerki russkoj dialektologii I*. Moscow.

Bamgboṣe, Ayọ, 1965. "Assimilation and Contraction in Yoruba", in *The Journal of West African Languages*, **2**: pp. 21–27.

Bloomfield, Leonard, 1939. "Menomini Morphophonemics", *TCLP*, **8**: pp. 105–15.

———, 1957. *Eastern Ojibwa*. Edited by Charles F. Hockett. Ann Arbor, Mich.

Brosnahan, L. F., 1964. "Outlines of the Phonology of the Gokana Dialect of Ogoni", in *The Journal of West African Languages*, **1**: pp. 43–48.

Burling, Robbins, 1966. "The Addition of Final Stops in the History of Maru", in *Language*, **42**: pp. 581–86.

Echeverría, Max S., and Heles Contreras, 1965. "Araucanian Phonemics", in *IJAL*, **31**: pp. 132–35.

Faust, Norma, and Evelyn G. Pike, 1959. "The Cocama Sound System", in *Publicações do Museo Nacional, Série Lingüistica Especial*, **1**: pp. 10–55.

Ferguson, Charles A., and Munier Chowdhury, 1960. "The Phonemes of Bengali", in *Language*, **36**: pp. 22–59.

Garvin, Paul L., 1950. "Wichita I: Phonemes", in *IJAL*, **16**: pp. 179–84.

Goodman, Morris, 1967. "Prosodic Features of Bravanese, A Swahili Dialect". Multilithed. Northwestern University.

Goodwin, William W., 1892. *A Greek Grammar*. Boston.

133

Grimes, Joseph E., 1959. "Huichol Tone and Intonation". *IJAL*, **25**: pp. 221–32.

Harms, Robert T., 1962. *Estonian Grammar* (identical with *Indiana University Publications Uralic and Altaic Series*, **12**). Bloomington, Indiana, and The Hague.

Harrell, Richard S., 1957. *The Phonology of Colloquial Egyptian Arabic.* New York.

Hodge, Carleton Taylor, 1947. *An outline of Hausa Grammar* (identical with *Language Dissertation No. 41*). Baltimore, Md.

Hohepa, Patrick W., 1967. *A Profile Generative Grammar of Maori. Indiana University Publications in Anthropology and Linguistics Memoir 20* (identical with *IJAL*, **33**, No. 2). Bloomington, Indiana.

Itkonen, Terho, 1964. *Proto-Finnic Final Consonants I : 1.* Helsinki.

Kensinger, Kenneth M., 1963. "The Phonological Hierarchy of Cashinahua (Pano)", in *Studies in Peruvian Indian Languages: I*: pp. 207–17. Edited by Benjamin F. Nelson. Norman, Oklahoma.

Key, Harold, 1961. "Phonotactics of Cayuvava", in *IJAL*, **27**: pp. 143–50.

Kinkade, M. Dale, 1966. "Vowel Alternation in Upper Chehalis", in *IJAL*, **32**: pp. 343–49.

Lehn, Walter, and Peter Abboud, 1965. "Beginning Cairo Arabic". Multilithed. Austin, Texas.

Levin, Norman Balfour, 1964. *The Assiniboine Language. Publication Thirty-two of the Indiana University Research Center in Anthropology, Folklore, and Linguistics* (identical with *IJAL*, **30**, No. 3, Part II). Bloomington, Indiana, and The Hague.

Mak, Cornelia. 1958. "The Tonal System of a Third Mixtec Dialect", in *IJAL*, **24**: pp. 61–70.

Mattingly, I. G., 1960. "The Phonemic Structure of Nootka", in *NSA Technical Journal: Special Linguistic Issue*: pp. 75–83.

Olmsted, D. L., 1958. "Atsugewi Phonology', in *IJAL*, **24**: pp. 215–20.

Osborn, Henry A., Jr., 1966. "Warao I: Phonology and Morphophonemics", in *IJAL*, **32**: pp. 108–23.

Paškov, B. K., 1963. *Manjčžurskij jazyk.* Moscow.

Percival, Keith, 1960. "A Problem in Competing Phonemic Solutions", in *Language*, **36**: pp. 383–86.

Postal, Paul M., 1964. "Boas and the Development of Phonology: Comments Based on Iroquoian", in *IJAL*, **30**: pp. 269–80.

Redden, James E., 1966. "Walapai I: Phonology", *IJAL*, **32**: pp. 1–16.

Riche, Furne, 1963. "Arabela Phonemes and High-Level Phonology", *Studies in Peruvian Indian Languages: I*: pp. 193–206. Edited by Benjamin F. Elson. Norman, Oklahoma.

Sapir, J. David, 1965. *A Grammar of Diola-Fogny* (identical with *West African Language Monographs 3*). Cambridge, England.

Sebeok, Thomas A., and Frances J. Ingemann, 1961. *An Eastern Cheremis Manual* (identical with *Indiana University Publications Uralic and Altaic Series*, **5**). Bloomington, Indiana, and The Hague.

Suárez, Jorge, A., 1959. "The Phonemes of an Araucanian Dialect", in *IJAL*, **25**: pp. 177–81.

Thompson, Laurence C., and M. Terry Thompson, 1966. "A Fresh Look at Tillamook Phonology", in *IJAL*, **32**: pp. 313–19.

Warotamasikkhadit, Udom, 1965. "A Phonological Grammar of Thai". Dittoed. Boston.

Williamson, Kay, 1965. *A Grammar of the Kolokuma Dialect of Ịjọ* (identical with *West African Language Monographs 2*). Cambridge, England.

Winter, Werner, 1966. "Yuman Languages II: Wolf's Son—A Walapai Text", in *IJAL*, **32**: pp. 17–40.

Language Index

137

Subject Index